Beyond the Bloom

LIFE LESSONS FROM THE MISADVENTURES OF A BEGINNER GARDENER

KELLY JACKSON CRABB

ISBN: 979-8-9933852-0-4

Edited by: MK Yeargin
Cover design: Kelly Crabb
Monarch illustration: Kim Koehler

For Jeremy, whose love is sunlight—
I bloom more fully because you planted yourself beside me,
and because you never stop believing in my becoming.

And to David and JJ, my favorite things to ever watch grow—
may you always stay curious and rooted,
and brave enough to cultivate what matters most to you.

*"And the day came when the risk
to remain tight in a bud
was more painful than the risk
it took to blossom."*

— Anaïs Nin —

CONTENTS

WHAT YOU'RE ACTUALLY HOLDING

Just to be clear: This is not a gardening how-to book. If you came for soil pH charts and Latin names, I promise you'll leave empty-handed. Instead, this is a book of stories shaped from and inspired by time I've spent in my garden.

If you don't know the difference between a dahlia and a delphinium, please know you're in excellent company. Neither did I when I started. Truthfully, you don't even have to like gardening to read this book, because this isn't a manual—it's a memoir. At its core, this is simply the story of a woman who decided to try something new. What matters here isn't the botany, it's the heart. The way dirt, sweat, and blisters somehow turned into perspective I couldn't have found anywhere else.

The garden has been my most surprising teacher. It has taught me about patience, resilience, and hope, as well as how grief and beauty can sit side-by-side like unlikely neighbors. It's where I learned that failure is compost for future joy, and that sometimes the scrappy little thing growing in the wrong place ends up being the miracle.

You'll also hear a lot about my life outside the garden in these pages—stories that connected me to what my garden was teaching along the way. My hope is that as you read, you'll somehow catch glimpses of your own life reflected back to you: the ways you're growing, the things that maybe need pruning, and the places you're being called to bloom, whether you're ready or not.

So don't worry about the color of your thumb. The only thing you need here is curiosity and a sense of humor when things go sideways. Wander through these pages like you would a slightly overgrown garden—expect a bit of chaos, but try not to miss the little moments of wonder. There's laughter here, as well as loss. There's also a whole lot of trial-and-error, more grace than I knew to expect, and way too many mistakes I could have avoided—but am awfully glad I didn't.

Underneath it all is this one stubborn truth: Waiting never grew me anything. Instead, the beauty came when I began. I hope this inspires you to begin as well, and to embrace the mess that comes with every start. Because honestly? The mess is half the fun.

CHAPTER ONE

THE ACCIDENTAL GARDENER

(OR ... BOTANICAL SIDE EFFECTS OF FALLING IN LOVE)

I don't think anyone is born with a green thumb. I believe a thumb becomes green simply by spending enough time in the dirt. Sometimes that happens by choice. Sometimes someone else's love of growing things rubs off on you. For me, though, it happened a little differently.

I fell in love at the ripe age of 37 after waiting (and waiting ... and waiting) for the right man to finally appear. He was more than I could have ever hoped for, even down to the detail of him being a package deal. When I fell in love, I not only found my soul mate but also became a stepmom to two incredible young boys. I also, coincidentally, gained a slobbery and fabulous Basset Hound named Maggie. It was the most unexpected path to family and also the most beautiful, perfectly timed gift.

I spent years watching friends fall in love and have children—albeit in a little less of an all-at-once kind of way, but ultimately always wanting the same for myself. Just when I thought all hope of one day having children myself was lost, I on-ramped into the wildest, most incredible "instafamily" experience I could have never seen coming.

I've had enough friends who came from blended families—and even spent a season as a youth pastor watching students navigate divorce—to know early on how much I needed to let their dad be their dad and their mom be their mom. Stepping into this role wasn't about replacing anyone; it was about being an extra dose of love, support, and stability for David and JJ. It also gave me the chance to free Jeremy from some of the grind of single parenting every other week so he could show up more fully as the playful, present dad he wanted to be. I knew the gift I'd been given: a front-row seat to these boys' lives, even while I was still very unfamiliar to them. Since "evil stepmother" was about the last vibe I wanted to channel, I made intentional choices early on to be present without being too pervasive.

I vividly remember in our newlywed days how the boys would ask their dad to play catch or basketball outside. Though I could have chosen to feel left out, I decided instead to simply be nearby—outside, but not in the way. I wanted them to have the best relationship with their dad, and I didn't want to force myself in, but I did want them to grow up knowing I was always there, quietly cheering, slowly and carefully earning their love and trust. You can only sit on a porch step for so long, however, before you start feeling a bit weird about it, so I started pulling weeds or trimming bushes, every now and again shouting out "Great catch!" or "Wow, that was fast!" Thanks to the massive pin oak in our front yard, I had an endless supply of dead leaves under the azaleas and rhododendrons to keep me busy, always taking the occasional break to clap or cheer when I spied a great free throw. Were these yard chores I naturally felt drawn to do? Not at all. But I wanted the boys to grow up remembering me in these moments, so I found myself, very unintentionally, putting my hands in the dirt.

We moved about 18 months into our marriage to a house that had a bigger yard and, conveniently, more weeds. As the boys grew, so did their desire to play more outside. Their dad was always eager to play catch and shoot hoops, so I therefore had many opportunities to be in the scene by tending to our landscaping. At this point, I started planting a few things here and there—always killing more than I would keep alive. But little by little, as things would make it, I would have more to do outside. The more they played, the more I planted. I not only ended up growing my connection with them but, coincidentally, cultivated an interest in gardening.

I never would have expected that becoming a stepmom would be the reason my thumb would turn green, but sure enough, it was. Combine a desire to be outside (for me, because of the boys), a willingness to keep trying regardless of failure (my parents instilled this in me), and a sense of curiosity (one of the ways I'm hardwired), and you can definitely get a long way in a garden.

When I started bravely putting things in the ground, I had zero idea what I was doing. Yet slowly but surely, I began feeling more drawn to the process. It felt like an invitation to co-creation. I would do my best to get something into the ground correctly and tend to it while it established roots, but I knew, in the end, the outcome wasn't really mine to control. Somewhere in that quiet rhythm of watering, watching, and waiting, something shifted. I began to believe in beauty I couldn't self-orchestrate and in possibilities I couldn't plan. And then came the summer after we moved into our new home, when I bought what I now refer to as "my magic celosia"—and I've never quite been the same ever since.

I popped into a local grocery store one of the hottest days of the year, the kind of Kansas City heat that feels like walking into a damp oven. I was only there for a watermelon, but right outside the entrance sat a sad little lineup of flower starters, baking in the sun like they were on death row. Only a few packs remained, drooping under a giant yellow 90% off sign, practically begging for rescue. For less than a dollar, I scooped up three. I then headed home, watermelon in one arm and clearance plants in the other, ready to tuck them into the front landscaping beds and see if I could revive them.

Celosia is a beautifully bizarre, rather Dr. Seuss-y plant, and much more my style than the mums we used to have as I was growing up. Plus, my mom impressed upon me how to both spot a good deal and stretch a dollar. Big sale signs set off a near-unconscious internal reaction, causing me to instinctively do the mental math without even realizing it. I knew it would have been downright silly to leave them behind for less than a dollar. If nothing else, they deserved to be tucked into the earth and given a big, long drink of water. I waited until dusk, settled them into their new home, and did as I always do, planting something new: prayed they would thrive despite my shortcomings.

Little did I know what would follow.

That summer, they did … okay. If I recall correctly, a couple died off after transplant, but I managed to keep most of them alive despite the late-season planting in the morbid summer heat. When the first frost came, they bid farewell as expected, and we pulled them out of the ground.

Or so I thought.

A few months later, in May 2017, we got to work in our landscaping beds, putting out fresh mulch and planting a couple of new things for the season. Not a week had passed before little green shoots started popping through the mulch. My husband was so annoyed. If you mulch your own garden beds, you can for sure understand his frustration. The amount of manual labor that goes into it all for the mere few days of pristine beauty that seem to follow just isn't a fair tradeoff (in my humble opinion).

Nevertheless, we persisted. We patiently pulled each tiny green shoot by hand, and then sure enough, a short handful of days later, they reappeared. We meticulously got to work pulling them again, only to have them pop up once more. Eventually, we caved and just let them be, allowing them to grow. We soon realized what they were as little tufts of color started surfacing at the tops. They weren't weeds as we originally suspected. They were little baby celosia sprouts! And they weren't just where I had planted the starters the summer before. They were *everywhere*. Hundreds of little shoots were surfacing, growing taller and larger than the year prior. I was dumbfounded because, well … they were labeled as annuals.

I spent all summer watching them grow, amazed every day not simply by their return, but by the way they were morphing into something altogether new. The bizarre shapes, the variety of colors … they were more unique and diverse than what grew the past summer. As a person whose main hope had been simply to keep what I planted alive, I had no idea that pollinators could help create something altogether new and different. I held a unique privilege of watching the celosia change and evolve with every shoot that bloomed. It welled up awe within me. Sometimes I looked at them and thought about how I originally found them, sun-parched and sold for pennies. Yet here they were now, multiplying and spreading in ways I didn't know were even possible, being cross-pollinated to become something ever-changing right in my very own yard. I found it all so remarkable, mystical, and utterly enchanting.

The following summer, in 2018, they sprouted again and covered even more of the landscaping bed, growing more bizarre than the year before. Apparently, they were reseeding themselves, a novel concept to this novice gardener. The label on the starter pack may have said "annual," but the flowers responded, "We ride at dawn." Their relentless comeback still feels like absolute magic to me.

Celosia got me hooked. I was captivated by the experience and couldn't get enough. I kept trying to plant additional things—still failing more than I succeeded. My garden beds became my living laboratory. The beautiful experiment of it all led me to new levels of wonder and delight. Every new thing I put in the ground became an opportunity to learn about light and water and how much healthy soil matters. I planted things that required full sun in mostly shaded areas, as well as shade plants in full sun—not on purpose, but because I was learning. I thought I understood what was required for each plant, but then I would find myself curious as to why certain things didn't work.

Every failure would lead to a deeper understanding. Every wilted bloom or browned leaf would make me search out answers. "Failure," as my friend Beth says, "is such a good teacher." I discovered what thrived in specific places and then found myself afraid to plant them anywhere else (or anything else in their place, for that matter). I must have tried five or six different things before gomphrena became the plant that thrived in this one tricky spot in my front landscaping bed. I had never seen anything take to that spot before, so it has officially become the space where gomphrena gets planted every year.

Celosia lit the fuse, and suddenly, my little garden experiments started spreading into every corner of the yard. Once you've had a taste of that kind of goodness, you can't help but go looking for more.

My next big lesson came from the shade garden project of 2019. We had a trampoline in our backyard that created just enough shade for a couple of hostas to go bonkers. The former homeowners had established them in the southwestern corner of the backyard, but a tree died there shortly after we moved in, leaving us no option but to cut it down. In doing so, this created too much light for the hostas to thrive. Who would have guessed a trampoline would be the secret-weapon gardening tool that made our hostas take off again? Completely inadvertently, mind you.

When we had to move the trampoline to a different part of the yard, I found myself nervous that we would kill the hostas. I now understood enough about light to see the trampoline's key role in creating their ideal environment, so we decided to transplant them and create a new shade garden on the north side of our house. By this point, they were ginormous and needed to be split, as did a few in another area.

So I picked up some ferns, coral bells, and hellebores at the local plant nursery, and we got to work. In the matter of an afternoon, we filled in a fairly abandoned area that runs along a pretty busy street. I have never seen the hostas we transplanted happier than they are now in our shade garden. People often comment as they walk by, "Nice hostas!" We even had someone shout it through their open car window once as they drove past us. Weird, I know. The satisfaction these compliments bring is definitive proof we are both old and not cool anymore, but hey … they're not wrong.

I kept learning as we tried new things. I figured out how to grow succulents and then transplant them inside. By the end of the summer, they were too lush and gorgeous to let them die in our frigid Kansas City winters, and too pricey to consider reinvesting in them each year. Nearby, as I searched for a less expensive route to fill a planter we have in a very sunny spot, I discovered how beautiful portucala (moss rose) can be for about a week and a half, but then how annoying they are to deadhead for the rest of the summer—so much so that I have vowed never to plant them again.

We also tried our hands at a butterfly garden, planting a bunch of things like yarrow, coneflower, and butterfly bush in a small space off our driveway in hopes of inviting all the local butterflies to come and dine from a perfectly curated smorgasbord of butterfly goodness. Apparently, this was before I understood how much water those plants specifically needed, or was it the heavy clay soil we failed to amend? Regardless, it didn't take long for it all to die. I took mental notes about what didn't work and decided to try again sometime, never letting failure be the end of the story.

Somehow, through all the false starts and trying again, our yard took shape, and people began commenting more and more about our beautiful landscaping. Since I now basically dream of having our property look like a botanical garden, I've become more aware of what else I want to be planting. I perhaps hadn't stopped long enough to fully realize just how far things had come along the way.

Through it all, though, no matter how much I may or may not have noticed, that thumb of mine kept growing ever greener. Not because I had some grand plan, but because I kept showing up—to weed, to plant, to fail, and to try again. Somewhere between the magic celosia's comeback tour and the long list of plants that didn't survive, the yard stopped being simply a yard. It became proof that growth is possible in the most unexpected places.

It turns out, the girl who once grabbed flowers because they were 90% off was now rearranging her weekends around plant shopping and plotting entire landscape takeovers. And honestly? I regret nothing.

CHAPTER TWO

FLOWERS FOR EZRA

IN MEMORY OF EZRA, 2004-2022

During the summer of 2022, the son of a college friend of mine was battling leukemia for the second time. I woke up at all times of the night thinking about him and his family, praying for his healing. It's so hard to watch people face things like they were, and it's so human to want to help—to somehow create a bit of lightness in an impossible situation. I knew firsthand from my own grief experience that nothing really could be done. Still, I ached to do something.

One morning, wide awake at 4:30 a.m. with my thoughts fixed on them, I got out of bed and started weeding my front landscaping beds. After years of pulling weeds just to keep an eye on the boys while they played, I had learned it could be equal parts annoying and therapeutic. That morning, though, it was definitely the latter— a quiet expression of what I like to call 'controlling the controllables,' something I cling to when life feels impossibly heavy.

As I sat pulling weed after weed, I kept wondering what I could do— even though I knew so little could actually be done. And that's when I looked up and saw the deep purple salvia and bright yellow daylilies, and a thought surfaced: *What if I made bouquets from all of this?*

In recent years, as my love of gardening had grown, so had my affection for arranging flowers—usually stems from Trader Joe's or Costco picked up during grocery runs, dropped into jars, and scattered around the house. I realized that morning, however, that after years of putting my hands in the dirt tending to these spaces, so much was accessible to me in my very own yard.

This idea began to take shape as a plan. I could share arrangements on social media, made from whatever was blooming that week, using vases and Mason jars I had tucked around the house. As people bought them, they could send a little donation directly to my friend Kirsten with the simple memo "Flowers for Ezra."

I didn't expect this to cure him. I didn't expect it to make a meaningful dent in medical bills. But maybe—just maybe—it could cover coffee on the way to the hospital. Or the ease of picking up a pizza for their other boys at home after a hard day. Or funds for a house cleaner now and then. Anything that brought them even a little dose of comfort as they faced the unimaginable.

The idea felt like one of those sacred whispers that quietly passes through your mind and then won't let go of your heart. Over time, that's how I've come to recognize God's voice in my life, so I paid close attention.

It didn't seem like much, but I decided to start simply cutting and arranging flowers. Honestly, isn't that how it often goes? The answer is often already right there in front of you. It's not always some grand reinvention. Sometimes it's just using what you have—or who you already are—for the good of someone else. It felt, in a way, like the botanical version of the Little Drummer Boy. I had no gold to bring, but I could offer this. And so I did.

The response utterly floored me. By how many people wanted to help. By how many and how much variety in arrangements came simply from what we had growing, in landscaping beds we had been developing over time. All those failed attempts that led to finding just the right things for just the right places were in full bloom—overflowing with possibility to be used for good. One by one, I would photograph what I had put together and post images online, thanking the person who ordered them. Those photos sparked curiosity in others to help a family face the unthinkable—a family whom most of them didn't even know.

After a while, I started getting so many orders that I wondered if I would run out of flowers to use. But wouldn't you know? A friend offered flowers from her garden, expanding what I could work with to include fresh, locally grown zinnias, amaranth, and a variety of celosia I had never seen before. I drove over with a bucket and garden snips, having been given free rein to take what I needed. I still remember pulling up and seeing it all in the late summer golden hour light, cosmos fluttering in the wind, and zinnias unfurling in layers of varied petals. I knew instantly, wide-eyed with wonder as I stood in that space, that I wanted to find room to grow something similar in our yard.

I'm convinced dreams are often born that quickly. Ironically, they are often discarded as soon as they surface. I was 47 years old and had never once thought of having my yard completely covered in flowers. Yet there I was, standing in my friend's garden, no longer seeing our landscaping beds as my boundaries. I wanted to rip up our grass and grow everything imaginable, and the more I pictured it in my mind, the more I knew it would become my reality.

I am a unique combination of dreamer and doer. I don't just want to sit around and think about things. I figure out the steps to make something happen and put that plan into action. Yet as a creative, I also dream lots of dreams, and it's oftentimes challenging to know exactly where to put my energy. I get impatient waiting to figure out what I should focus on with so many dreams fluttering about, but the older I get, the more I have learned to listen to my gut—and my gut was undeniably pulling me towards flowers.

I still find it crazy that the dream of flowers never surfaced during my 20s or 30s. It all came later in life (arguably at just the right time) and through being willing to explore the unknown, regardless of outcome. One thing was certain: I wasn't going to figure it out by doing nothing. I determined that I wouldn't let the fear of failure or the belief I had to figure everything out before I began steer the process. Instead, I gave the keys to adventure and curiosity and decided to see where they led me. Not everything has to make sense to be worth trying. Dreams don't always need blueprints. Sometimes soil will do.

Around this point, someone asked if I was familiar with Erin Benzakein, a flower farmer committed to organic and sustainable agriculture located in the Pacific Northwest. Apparently, she was all the rage amongst flower fans, but I always tend to be late to the party, so it was no surprise to me that I had not yet heard of her. After a quick scroll through her Instagram page (@floretflower), I was all in. Her photos, her knowledge, her approach … I couldn't get enough. I spent hours studying her posts, soaking up everything I could. The more I learned, the more serious I got about the dream that had started to take root in me. I wanted a space of my own to grow cut flowers. Badly. I couldn't stop reading, planning, hoping—trying to figure out how to make it real.

Naturally, I decided the only logical thing to do was create a new space on our lot, right smack in the middle of suburbia, and mark my calendar for Erin's upcoming seed sale. I heard things sold quickly, so I set a phone alert like I was trying to score Justin Timberlake tickets. And there I was on the day of the seed drop, Floret's website open, ready to panic-click my way through the sale. My plan? Add anything that looked remotely interesting to my cart. Which, in practice, meant one of everything.

Mind you, I don't think I'd even told my husband I wanted to start a cut flower garden at this point. In fact, I can say with confidence I had not. Which felt important, considering he had only recently dug up 40 square feet of grass with a shovel and his bare hands to help me plant what turned out to be a failed butterfly garden—the very spot, in fact, where I was now imagining my future mini flower farm.

Can we just pause for a moment to laugh at what I considered the next *logical* step here? The 40-square-foot butterfly garden, full of well-established plants from a trusted local nursery, hadn't worked out. Clearly, the solution was to expand that plot to 500 square feet and attempt to grow everything from seed. Obviously.

By Thanksgiving 2022, my excitement had welled up so much that I couldn't keep the secret anymore and spilled every single bean to Jeremy. A few weeks later, I discovered garden snips and one of Erin's books in my Christmas stocking, compliments of my husband. He is consistently my number one supporter, always on the ready to help my dreams come to life—so when I told him I wanted to plant a cut flower garden, he didn't hesitate one bit. Instead, he filled my Christmas stocking with the tools I would need. There wasn't even a mere mention of the failed butterfly garden—just his unwavering belief that I could do it.

The following March, Jeremy and I headed to Spain to celebrate our tenth anniversary. On the transatlantic flight back, I stumbled across the first episode of *Growing Floret*, a short docuseries about Erin Benzakein and her farm. Who knew this was even a thing? (Again, always late to the party.) I sat there, as most everyone slept around me, mesmerized and completely delighted to be starting the show.

Within minutes, tears uncontrollably started flowing down my face. I wasn't emotionally prepared for how that docuseries tapped into a previously unknown part of my soul. Neither was the stranger sitting to my right. (Sorry, man.) Even still, that pull within kept growing, along with my curiosity and desire to explore more of what this might be, and it all started to feel more like something to which I was being called. I sat watching, dreaming, listening, planning, and allowed the awakening in me to expand.

Something shifted in me at 30,000 feet, and I wasn't about to keep it to myself. So naturally, the first thing I did—jet lag and all—was cue it up again and make Jeremy watch the entire first season of *Growing Floret* with me.

It might come as a surprise, but while watching that first episode of *Growing Floret*, Jeremy also got emotional. Truthfully, he gets emotional watching *American Idol* and animal videos on Instagram (one of the things I find most endearing about him). But as I saw that first tear fall from his eyes while Erin and her husband's story unfolded, I knew he wasn't just going to support this dream. He was going to help me build it.

The next day, I ordered seed trays, grabbed bags of soil labeled "Seed Starting" (seemed foolproof), and laid out every last packet from the *Floret Seed Sale* like a treasure map. I took one slightly dramatic breath and leapt in with the confidence of someone who has no idea what she's doing—enthusiasm, however, cranked to full throttle. In my mind, I was already morphing into an Erin Benzakein minion—overalls and all—running a suburban flower empire from our cul-de-sac. It was a flawless plan. What could possibly go wrong?

Looking back, I can see how something that started as a desperate 4:30 a.m. attempt to "do something" for a hurting family became the spark that lit an entirely new path for me. One act of using what I already had—in this case, some flowers, a few jars, and a willingness to ask—opened the door to a dream I didn't even know was in me.

That's the sneaky way dreams work sometimes. They don't always arrive as a lightning bolt or a carefully drafted five-year plan. Sometimes they tiptoe in, disguised as a middle-of-the-night idea, as a small act of kindness, or as something you do simply because you can. And if you say yes—if you take that first, wobbly step—you may just find yourself in a garden that's bigger and wilder than anything you could have plotted on paper.

For me, it started with a handful of bouquets in jars. It grew into an entire reimagining of my yard, my priorities, and my life. I couldn't have told you then that Flowers for Ezra would lead to a micro flower farm in our suburban lawn, but here we are.

So here's my advice: Don't wait until you have the perfect step-by-step plan. Use what you've got, where you are, for whoever needs it. The most beautiful things you'll ever grow might just start with giving away what you already have. And sometimes, if you're lucky, they'll take over your whole yard.

CHAPTER THREE

WELL, THAT DIDN'T GO AS PLANNED

Let's be really clear about something: Experience has always been my greatest teacher. It's one of the things my parents commented about enough times as I was growing up that I can still hear both of their voices in my head telling me, "You don't have to learn everything the hard way." And yet … I did. Being almost 50 and a stepmother of two, I now understand why they were always trying to help me avert the steep learning curve I chose for myself. God bless them, they sure did try. It's just always how I've learned best.

I believe deeply that almost everything in life is "figureoutable." I also place learning how to pivot and correct mid-process as a crucial life skill. When you dive in without always thinking everything through or doing enough research, you're presented with many an opportunity to put problem-solving skills to the test. This way of learning, combined with my hyper-developed fear of failure, has led me over time to harness one of life's most important qualities: grit. Some might call it stubbornness (this is me looking at you, Jeremy), but I prefer to believe it's grit. When you add up someone's levels of courage, resilience, and resolve, you discover exactly how gritty they are—and starting a cut flower garden quickly provides a fantastic way to put that grit through the paces.

Which brings me to the seed-starting debacle of 2023. As I recovered from jet lag after returning home from Spain, with our dining room table full of seed starting supplies, my excitement far outweighed my exhaustion. I got to work nestling all the various seeds in their trays and took them down to our basement. There, Jeremy and I tied up grow lights to a wire shelf and set up a little portable heater we owned to try to raise the temperature of the space to 70 degrees. I figured that little heater would work just the same as the fancy pants heat mats most flower farmers use for germination. For the record, it did not. OSHA would not approve my methods. Meanwhile, I also didn't put the grow lights on a timer. In fact, I failed to do enough homework to know they needed to mimic the timing of the sun (whoopsiedoodle). Though looking back, that makes a ton of sense. So there my first seeds started their growth journey, a bit chilly and overstimulated.

And yet … they grew. I think most of nature has a strong will to not only survive, but to grow. There are limits to that, sure. But I am finding through this journey that nature will find a way, not because of us, but despite us. Thank God.

I remember going down to the basement every day, sometimes every couple of hours, to watch little seedlings sprout out of the soil. Not all of them did, probably because of the light and heat issues, or maybe they were too far down in the soil to begin with—because apparently that's a thing too. But hey, I wasn't going to have enough room for all of them to be transplanted outside anyway. I planned for and expected a certain level of failure, so the ones who made their way out and started showing signs of life gave me such a thrill.

As they grew, the first of many issues that would come started presenting itself. Some sprouts would shrivel when they didn't have enough water—or had too much. Some would turn black, probably because I was doing nothing to feed them (apparently, fertilizer goes a long way in this process, even from the very beginning). Some would grow a bit and then lose all ability to stand upright—who even knows why? Some got "leggy" since not only was I leaving the lights on all the time, but they were also way too far away from the seed trays. I literally did just about everything wrong that I possibly could. Yet on

Memorial Day weekend, on a 92-degree day, I somehow had enough itty-bitty, teeny-weeny seedlings to transplant out to the garden.

Had I "hardened them off," you might ask? Short answer: Absolutely not. Long answer: Also absolutely not, since hardening off seedlings requires a slow, deliberate transition from the safety of their indoor growth to the unpredictable conditions of being outside. That would have required weeks! I started this process late, and it was getting super hot already that May, so I figured we could just skip over that part. (Sorry, Erin Benzakein. I know you told me to, but I decided I would try it another way. You know … because I like to learn everything the hard way.)

Allow me to humor you with another huge blunder I made as we prepped for transplant day. (This is a good one.)

Jeremy, being the quintessential architect, loves any opportunity he is given to use graph paper or X-acto knives. Once we had a decent idea of how many seedlings were going to survive and be ready to transplant, he subsequently sketched a layout of the space we'd set aside in the yard so I could map out which varieties would go where.

He was convinced we didn't have nearly enough room in our original plan, while I—shocking to no one—thought we should just wing it. And yet he persisted. I mean, he's *real* cute—and, as a result, can get away with being a lot more persuasive with me than anyone else ever could. As we worked up how many zinnia seedlings could fit in one corner and how much amaranth could fit in another, it became painfully clear how much Jeremy was (sigh) right. I absolutely needed at least twice the space we had originally considered. Cool. Cool, cool, cool.

When we went outside and marked the expanded space off in our yard with stakes and twine to visualize what it would look like, I immediately thought, "Our neighbors are going to hate us." (Maybe they do. They haven't told me.) Since the area that gets the most sun in our yard through the day is right next to our driveway, so this wasn't going to be a little garden at all, let alone one tucked away in the backyard. Instead, it was going to be massive and highly, highly visible.

I know I could have adjusted my plan, but I just couldn't imagine letting any of these little-seedlings-that-could get thrown out. They had made it this far, despite my best efforts. They should at least have the chance to grow, right? So we went for it. Since my mode of operation most of the time tends to look a lot like *go big or go home* (see also: the rest of this book), that is exactly what we did.

The following weekend, Jeremy rented a machine at Home Depot and pulled up roughly 500 square feet of sod. Since we're gluttons for punishment, we also moved said sod to another area in our yard in need of healthier grass. Have you ever rolled up and hauled sod across your yard? Zero stars. Do not recommend. We were literally sore for *days*.

When it was all said and done, I looked at the newly prepped area for my cut flower garden and immediately thought, "What the hell have we done?" The failed butterfly garden looked like child's play compared to this. I stared at the massive stretch of bare earth, praying I hadn't just made one of the biggest mistakes of my life—and forced Jeremy to promise that if it flopped, he wouldn't hold it against me forever.

Meanwhile, I ordered seven cubic yards of organic compost to be delivered the following weekend. Seven. Cubic. Yards. Guys, that's *a lot* of dirt. It's about 65 wheelbarrows worth, to be exact, which means your arms are going to look like you've been training for *American Ninja Warrior* by the time you're done moving it. We carefully distributed it over the 500 square feet of bare ground (and by we, I mean Jeremy) and then just let it sit there.

Did we amend it with the existing soil? Nope. Was this particular compost one that looked and behaved more like mulch? You betcha. I'll let you imagine how terribly matched my itty-bitty, teeny-weeny seedlings were with the texture of this specific compost. It was like trying to make cooked spaghetti noodles stand upright in a bowl of Shredded Wheat. There was absolutely no grip to hold anything in place. The more we transplanted them in the ground and watched the non-hardened-off, itty-bitty, teeny-weeny seedlings wilt in the

92-degree heat, the more I knew what a terrible series of choices had been made (by me … I blame no one but me).

"Maybe I should have done a little more homework," I thought to myself.

"Ya think?" my inner critic sarcastically clapped back.

The next day, I walked out to the most pathetic-looking garden and just prayed as I exhaled, "Lord, have mercy." What was done was done. It was in Jesus' hands now. (And honestly? I think he even sighed a little.) Since it was going to be miserably hot the first week these plant babies were in the ground, I knew they would need water. Scratch that. I *assumed* they would need water.

It became my routine to pray for these baby seedlings as I watered them. I knew there was so little I could do at this point and began the work of opening my hands and surrendering the outcome. You know those times in life when you hold onto something so tightly, all you end up with is bloody palms from digging your nails in as you grip? This was definitely not one of them for me. I had but one shred of hope that came from my friend April, who had once shared her garden with me back when I was arranging Flowers for Ezra. After telling her all the mistakes I had made, she simply said, "Something will grow. It won't all grow, but something will."

So, for the flowers that would make it, I would go out daily and water them. I would weed. I would read up on how to fertilize them. (I was finally doing some homework!) My phone figured out what I was searching for on the web and started sharing Instagram ads for me as I scrolled. That tricky little algorithm knew I was looking for organic options, so it gave me the hard press for some very eco-friendly products every time it could.

Eventually, I succumbed to the endless ads I was being presented with and ordered a starter set from a company called Bug Hut. A few days later, a collection of very well-branded bottles showed up and we got to work using them.

It had been about a month. Every night when Jeremy would come home from work, we would walk around the perimeter of the garden, inspecting each area closely for any little sign of growth. The fact they hadn't all died off in and of itself was a miracle, but they were literally showing zero growth whatsoever. Nada. Zip. Zilch. I wondered if I should give up on it all. I *wanted* to give up on it all.

I felt like a fool standing by my failure-to-thrive garden every night, faithfully watering those poor little seedlings, hoping things would take off. I drove to my favorite local flower nursery to talk to someone who might know what to do. At one point, I even reached out to a local flower farmer, and she was pretty convinced it was doomed, too. Skipping the step of mixing the compost with the existing soil might have been where all hope died.

Yet just after it seemed nothing was going to do anything, the first signs of growth appeared. I still remember the very first zinnia that surfaced. It was the ugliest, most pathetic-looking flower in the history of flowers, but to me it was an absolute wonder. I celebrated that little zinnia so hard. I cheered and whooped and hollered and probably even danced a little. I couldn't contain my excitement when Jeremy arrived home, so I made him run out to see it. We were equally delighted and popped some champagne in its honor. It was objectively homely, but I treated it like the freaking Met Gala. And yet, the next day, when I went back to check and see if it had grown anymore, it had completely fallen over because it was so top-heavy. The weak, little stem couldn't even support its pathetic little floret. I felt like such a failure. I couldn't even get a zinnia to grow. A zin-ni-a, for crying out loud. (For those of you unfamiliar, zinnias essentially grow like weeds.)

That I kept going still astounds me. I have given up on much more important things by this point in the game. But I kept considering April's sentiment that something was going to grow. It wouldn't all grow, but something would. The hope of *what could be* kept me going, no matter how much like a fool I looked standing in that pathetic garden every day, believing something might come from it all.

Here's the truth: My garden *was* growing—we just couldn't see it. It was growing and establishing roots deep in the soil below, long before it ever showed signs of growth above ground. It was doing the invisible work of survival, the underground hustle no one celebrates. (There is, tragically, no applause for roots.) While I was pacing around the yard questioning every choice I'd made, those tiny seedlings were busy establishing roots. Quietly. Persistently. Unapologetically slow.

For goodness' sake, considering we'd dumped three to five inches of pure compost on top of the actual soil (bless it), those roots had a lot more ground to cover than your average seedlings. They had to muscle through a dense layer of compost. Those plants had to dig deep—*really* deep—before they ever had a chance of standing tall. And it turns out, the taller you hope to grow, the deeper you have to root. (Noted.)

I started thinking about all the times I've tried to jump ahead to the blooming part—when I've wanted the joy, the fruit, the harvest *now*—without doing the patient, often boring work of laying a foundation. It's so human, isn't it? We rush to be seen, to succeed, to sparkle … but roots aren't flashy. They're hidden, slow, and require consistency. Tragic, I know.

And yet, rooting is everything. It's how we're stabilized when the storms come. It's how we pull in what we need to grow. It's how we stay anchored when the winds of opinion, failure or comparison try to knock us sideways.

I realized the garden wasn't just teaching me how plants grow. It was reminding me how *people* grow, how *I* grow. How every version of myself that's ever endured something hard had to root down before I could rise up. How much damage can be done when you try to bloom before you're ready—when you try to build something beautiful without first deciding what you'll stand on. Whether it be with faith, core values, or your integrity, the foundation upon which you build your life matters, and it takes time.

We live in a world that rewards the visible: the shiny success, the blooming moment. But I'm learning to celebrate what's happening beneath the surface. In the quiet. In the dark. In the unseen. Because that's where real strength is forged. Shiny is nice, but sturdiness is necessary.

Root first.
Then bloom.
Every time.

CHAPTER FOUR

SMELLS LIKE PROMISE

One day that first summer, our super cute neighbor kids ran over while I was working in the garden—right after I'd applied some fish emulsion.

"What is that *smell*?!" they asked, gagging.

I figured the word emulsion would fly right over the heads of an 8- and 5-year-old, so with a mischievous grin, I said, "Oh, I just watered the garden with some liquefied fish guts."

Their eyes nearly popped out of their heads. "Why don't you just use water?!" they demanded. I launched into a half-explanation, but before I could finish, they shrieked, "Fish guts?! BLECH!" and sprinted back home, noses plugged.

Honestly, fair. It smells like death in a bottle, but holy cow, does it ever work. I remember the praise for fish emulsion on *Growing Floret*, basically calling it liquid gold. They're not wrong. It's absolute magic, but it's also the color of diarrhea and smells like a dockside dumpster in July, so consider yourself warned.

I wasn't even sure what was in the bottles I ordered from Bug Hut. I just followed the directions (go me!) after seeing rave reviews. One was for root growth. Another promised protection from heat. And then there was this one, for "nutrition."

Pretty sure I also gagged the first time I opened it. "This has to be fish emulsion," I thought, eyes watering.

Whose idea was this, anyway? Who originally thought they should puree fish guts, believing it would be an ideal fertilizer … for flowers? Regardless, I swear it turned the ship around. My poor little seedlings, stagnant for a month, suddenly took off after my first couple of applications. Turns out, plants need more than just water and sunshine. They also need nourishment, so I will never skip a week of feeding my seedlings again. As in, never ever.

Soon thereafter, many of my seedlings hit a point in growth where I needed to "pinch" them. To clarify, this was not a cute little playful pinch. This was a ruthless cutting you give your plants when they're only eight to twelve inches tall—often before they even bud. I had read about this on the back of some seed packets, and Erin had explained it in one of her workshops. But imagine how hard it was for me to go into a garden I had just recently stopped believing was doomed and cut back all of the growth except the bottom couple sets of leaves on each stem. I might have actually cried.

Pinching is something gardeners do with many cut-and-come-again flowers to force them to grow several blooming branches versus only one. It feels so counterintuitive, but it is an essential step to making a garden ridiculously productive. So I pulled out the snips Jeremy gifted me in my stocking at Christmas, trusted the process, and got to work.

As I snipped my way through the garden, I kept hesitating, hovering my shears over stem after stem. It felt wrong, cutting something that finally showed signs of growth. However, I'd read enough to know what would happen if I didn't: The plants would stretch tall, but put all their energy into one bloom. No branching. No abundance.

I couldn't help but think ... isn't that life sometimes? We grow something—a dream, a role, a version of ourselves—and it oftentimes feels like progress, like momentum. Then something (or someone, or even God) asks us to cut it back, to let go of what looks good in order to make space for what's better. It's disorienting. Painful, even. But maybe surrendering the growth we thought we wanted allows something deeper, fuller, and more resilient to take shape instead.

I lived out this reality back in 2018 when nerve issues in my neck forced me into early retirement as a professional photographer. Talk about a doozie. I had no Plan B, no current resume, and newfound restrictions from my neurologist that left me wondering what I could possibly do for work. When you're told to "not sit at a desk or lift more than 10 pounds," what's even left? I remember thinking, "Perfect! I'll just hover in the void and do nothing. That'll pay the bills."

Photography had been my life's work for over 20 years—until almost overnight, I was told it was time to pivot. It felt cruel and unfair. I couldn't yet see where it was leading. All I knew was that everything I'd built was being cleared away. Yet, unbeknownst to me, beneath that disruption, something new was being formed. I was being given an unexpected new route that would allow me to bloom differently than I ever imagined.

After I'd made my way through pinching everything in the garden, I looked over what felt like a floral massacre, a bag of what "once was" in my hand, and sighed. Pinching was definitely not my favorite part of this process. It felt like ten steps back after thinking I was getting somewhere.

I quickly realized it was time for that week's application of fish guts. I filled up my watering can, added the precise amount of fish emulsion to create the magic sauce, and headed out to the garden to stink everything up. As I poured those liquefied fish guts over my annihilated garden, I found myself thinking about how sometimes the stinkiest situations cause the most growth. Like having to retire unexpectedly from a 20-year career. The news had been downright foul. The fish-guts kind of foul.

It makes it easier to handle the pain of loss and the stink of hard situations when you know the potential for beauty comes from it all, doesn't it? When I look back at the forced career pivot, the heartbreaks, and the disappointments that made me want to curl up and quit—I see now that every one of those moments became the catalyst for something new. Not always immediately. Not always easily. But inevitably, something always grew.

After enough hindsight moments (which almost all 50-ish-year-olds simply have due to the sheer amount of life lived), I've begun to trust that hard does not always equal bad. I don't necessarily *welcome* hard by any means, but I now know that growth isn't always gentle. It doesn't always feel good. Sometimes it requires cutting things that seem healthy. Sometimes it involves nourishing yourself in ways that make you gag a little. Sometimes the road to blooming is just downright messy and wild and kind of absurd.

I always allow myself to feel what I need to as I face it. You just must. There's no avoiding disappointment or sadness. So, I take a minute and turn my nose up at it. I give myself a moment to say whatever version of "Fish guts! Blech!!" I need to based on what I'm facing. Maybe I even try to run away from it all, like my neighbor kids did while closing their noses with their little fingers. However, I truly want to be someone who says, "Ok. Now that we've got all that done, let's sit back and wait for the blooming." Because sometimes the most fertile ground is born of broken things.

Expect it.
Look for it.
Beauty is coming.

A few days later, the smell finally faded. (Praise be.) The garden still looked like a crime scene—just short stubs where tall stems used to be—but I trusted it knew what it was doing, even if I still wasn't entirely sure I knew what *I* was doing.

I wandered through with my coffee in one hand and a vague sense of optimism in the other, squinting for signs of life. Sure enough, there they were—tiny bits of green already pushing out from where I'd made the cuts. It wasn't dramatic. Nothing bloom-worthy. Nothing I could post on Instagram with a poetic caption and a filtered sunrise. Just the quiet, gritty, sometimes slightly ridiculous work of becoming.

So I held on, knowing that sometimes growth looks like forward momentum. Sometimes it looks like (or smells like) death. More often than not, however, it looks stubby, awkward, smelly, and slow—yet still, somehow, full of promise.

CHAPTER FIVE

ORGANIC OR BUST

(AND OTHER THINGS I THOUGHT I'D NEVER SAY)

If you had told me a decade ago that I'd end up standing in my backyard, braless, greeting bees like a suburban Snow White in overalls and a black tank top, I would have laughed you straight out of the room. And yet, here we are.

The hippy-dippy slide for me started in the most unexpected way. In 2018, right after being told to officially retire from lugging my camera equipment around like a pack mule, an opportunity fell out of the sky to become a wine rep for a startup devoted to sustainability and organic farming. Even typing that conjures up the super sexy feelings I had about becoming part of the wine world. Suddenly, I was strutting around in my mind like some chic sommelier who could casually pair the perfect wine with your Enneagram number. Très fancy. Très glamorous.

Surprisingly? I kind of loved the idea. It was a big leap from my life as a photographer, but the startup's mission to care for the planet and back small family growers didn't just sound good—it *felt* good. Plus, wine has this sneaky little superpower of pulling people together around a table, causing them to linger longer and downshift for a bit. I mean ... say less. I pictured long nights on patios and around dining tables, laughter hanging in the air, and me telling the stories of small vineyards caring for the planet—and somehow calling it work. Most importantly, because a wine bottle weighs less than my purse, this new career would also be doctor-approved, thank you very much.

Meanwhile, we'd just moved into a house we adored, the boys were busy learning to drive and rock climb (while orthodontia bills rolled in with price tags high enough to buy a used Honda Civic), and Jeremy and I were dreaming big dreams of seeing the world. My doctor made it clear that pushing my body was non-negotiable, but we needed a second income to live the lives we were envisioning. After we prayed and believed God would make a way, the timing of this new opportunity felt like more than a coincidence. So—bada bing bada boom—I became a wine rep.

Did I know anything about wine? At that point, other than being able to distinguish between a white and a red, no. Did I let that stop me? Also, no, because when has that ever? What I did have was a willingness to be a beginner again, to nod knowingly at words like "tannins" while secretly wondering if it was a fancy way to say "bitter," and to trust, again, that everything tends to be figureoutable along the way. Not immediately, of course, but eventually.

Over the last seven years, I've swirled, sniffed, and learned to detect "notes of leather and crushed violets" (translation: smells like wine). I've met growers and winemakers whose stories made me cry. I've truly enjoyed the process of sharing what I've learned with others. I've also managed to get pretty good at the swirl-sniff-sip routine, usually without spilling it on myself—though half the time what I really smell is "grape" and maybe "fancy wood."

What I thought I signed up for was a flexible paycheck while I focused on physical therapy and caring for my body. What I actually got was a crash course in sustainable farming, as well as an army of incredible new friends. I've learned what happens when farmers love the soil, the crops, and the people tending them like they're part of the family. It's given me a deeper conviction that one single person can make a difference with small, consistent choices, not just for today, but for the future generations who end up inheriting this wild mess of ours.

The more I learned about sustainability, the more these values leaked into all sorts of crevices in my regular life. I started buying from companies with the same type of values (yes, as a matter of fact, we *do* use bamboo toilet paper). I found ways to cut down on waste and energy use at home (composting like a champ these days). And yes—I became that person who will pull a soda can out of the trash so I can move it to the recycling bin. I typically then give the offender *the look*—the one that says, "I'm not mad, just disappointed."—which, let's be honest, is far worse. Ten years ago, I would've laughed at the mental image. Now? It's just an ordinary Tuesday.

When I planted my first cut flower garden in 2023, it was very much a culmination of both spending time outside with my stepsons and the unexpected dream born out of Flowers for Ezra. I firmly believe, however, it was also in part because of the yes I said to becoming an organic wine rep several years earlier. That yes didn't just give me a paycheck—it rewired the way I paid attention. I'd learned to notice the small things, to care about how food (and wine) was grown, and to realize just how much life depends on pollinators—those tiny, winged rockstars keeping the world alive.

When it came time to dig into creating my cut flower garden, it wasn't just about pretty blooms. It was also about capturing beauty in a new way after putting my camera down—and doing it with intention. After years of selling organic wine and making one eco-conscious tweak at a time, I'd slid so far down the sustainability slope. By the time I planted cut flowers, I was fully committed to doing it organically and sustainably, inspired by so many of the farmers I had come to respect. Every decision, from the seeds I ordered to how I handled pests and treated disease, would go through the filter: *Will this help or harm the environment?*

In 2021, I made my first trip out to Sonoma and visited remarkable growers who lived by the same "organic or bust" philosophy. I asked questions, listened, and learned from people who had their boots in the dirt every single day. They were constantly up against something from drought and wildfires to pests and disease, yet their conviction to care for the planet never wavered. Even when it cost them personally, they always chose stewardship over shortcuts.

Two years later, I went back to California and had the privilege of visiting Golden Vineyards, a private estate in Mendocino County. Words fail to describe this incredible property adequately. It truly felt like being in a current-day Garden of Eden. Rolling hills, olive trees dripping with fruit, grapevines springing up through blooming cover crops—it was breathtaking. As I listened to stories about the demands of regenerative farming, I felt more inspired than I had in years—every intentional choice stacked upon another, building an ecosystem that actually hummed with life. Standing there, I couldn't shake the sense that this was how the world is intended to be.

As a result of these trips, I realized that while my flower crops *could* be much more abundant with the use of spray chemicals or synthetic fertilizers, the payoff would be short-lived. What I longed for instead was a garden teeming with life, not threatening it—just like these vineyards. I decided I'd rather have fewer blooms I could feel good about than an overflowing garden that came at the expense of the pollinators who make this kind of beauty possible.

In the early days, before I even knew whether anything would actually grow, I daydreamed of bees and butterflies drifting in like they'd found the buffet of their dreams. I imagined monarchs floating from stem to stem, bumblebees waddling down the rows, and me saying good morning like we were old friends. Was it a little utopian? Absolutely, but if talking to bees is wrong, I frankly don't want to be right.

Committing to this—*really* committing—meant making choices today that would matter tomorrow. Even when it would be harder. Even when it would be slower. Even when no one else would be standing in my backyard applauding me for doing it the "right" way.

That's true in the garden, and it's true everywhere else.

Know what you stand for before the first of anything happens—for me, that's when a seed hits the dirt. Because when the hard choices come—and they will—you won't have to overthink it or make a frantic pros-and-cons list. You'll already know.

For me, that plan is "organic or bust." No matter if it means fewer flowers or the garden takes its sweet time, I choose to say no to quick fixes or to "just this once" compromises. I've wholeheartedly decided the juice is worth the squeeze, and there's no talking me out of it.

Your version of "organic or bust" might not have anything to do with compost or pollinators. Maybe it's how you run your business, how you parent, or how you decide which humans get VIP access to your energy. It's whatever non-negotiables you plant deep enough that they grow through every decision, big or small.

Sure ... sometimes that means you'll watch other people bloom faster, fuller, and flashier. Sometimes you'll feel like the weirdo who brought organic, homemade kale chips to a Super Bowl party. But here's the truth: Sticking to your values is like weeding. It might not be fun at the moment, but it keeps the crap from choking out what you actually want to grow.

So decide on your version of "organic or bust"—whatever it is. Let it guide what you plant in your life, how you plant it, and from what you're willing to walk away. Because when your (figurative or literal) garden finally blooms—awkward, imperfect, a little wild—you'll know it's undeniably yours.

Cutting corners is a lot like eating Cheetos in white pants. Sure, you *can,* but you'll regret it instantly. Sticking to your values might take longer, but it also means you get to sleep at night and wake up proud of what you've grown.

Grow what matters.
Grow it in a way that matters.

And if the neighbors think you've lost it because you're outside braless, talking to bees—well, at least you've found yourself.

CHAPTER SIX

BEAUTY REQUIRES BOUNDARIES

Bunnies are only cute until they find their way to your garden and start treating it like their personal salad bar. For years, we have had bunnies in our yard, and I've always found them adorable. Never had I found them a nuisance until there were 500 square feet of baby plants at their disposal, and they wanted to eat just as much as I wanted to see my garden grow. Our youngest boy, a 15-year-old soon-to-be sophomore at the time, thought this would be the perfect opportunity to pull out his Papa's BB gun and "take care of the situation." Had we lived in the country … maybe. But I'm also a pacifist living in suburbia who has a soft spot for furry animals, so we decided a fence was probably our next best step and kept the BB gun safely tucked away.

At this point, my "little" flower garden had become an investment of well over a thousand bucks—simply to get going with zero promise of result. So when we had to start evaluating fence options, the goals were that it was 1) effective and 2) not a gazillion dollars. We also live in a fairly nice neighborhood, so we added 3) not an eyesore. After a quick skim of the home association bylaws, we determined that so long as it wasn't a chain link fence, we would be in the clear of any foreseeable fines or forcible removal. We found an option we felt achieved all the aforementioned goals and bit the bullet, investing a couple *more* hundred dollars in the project. (Between gardening and my love of travel, I think it's fair to say I need to find some less expensive hobbies.)

After careful perusal of all our options at the major home repair big box stores, we settled on some handy-dandy, three-foot-tall black plastic posts with metal tips, which would push easily into the ground with a little aid from a mallet. The rolls of black wire fencing we had chosen worked perfectly with them, and we got this thing put together super quickly—except about halfway through the install, we realized the plastic posts were not leaving the fence looking very straight. Instead, it was giving a much more "leaving the salon with a soft beach wave" vibe. This was definitely the fastest and perhaps cheapest way to get this done, but it also looked like it. So now we were the neighbors with a very visible, oversized garden surrounded by questionable fence choices. I'm sure if the neighbors didn't hate this project yet, this would send them over the edge.

We determined the only real option was to go back to Menards after removing our first attempt at "rabbit proofing" the garden, buy the steel stakes that cost twice as much, and attempt to install yet another fence, this time with a level. Neither of us was excited about the cost or time this would require, but with Jeremy being an architect and me caring a whole, whole lot about what the neighbors thought, driving up every day to a fence line that wasn't straight just wasn't going to fly. We got that second fence up without a hitch, and we were both much happier with the result.

Wait.
There was a hitch.
I'm sure you're not surprised.

My husband has joked for years now that he should get "C-A-L-L B-4-U-[line drawing of a shovel]" tattooed across his knuckles. This is because one year we decided to trust our failing 40-something-year-old brains to "remember" where the utility flags had been on previous projects, skip calling it in again, and rent a *power auger*. All to set a zipline post for the boys' birthdays. Genius, right? We did not, in fact, remember. Cue the entire surrounding neighborhood losing internet in the process. I'm still just grateful it wasn't the main power line. It's a long story, and I am definitely partially responsible, but it's fair to say we learned the hard way that you must *ALWAYS*, in fact, "C-A-L-L-B-4-U-[line drawing of a shovel]."

So, when I tell you that in the process of hammering these steel stakes for the new fence a couple of inches into the ground, we somehow managed to slice through our new Google Fiber line, would you find that as funny as we did? And by funny, I clearly mean *not funny*.

At this point, we should have surrendered and let the rabbits just feast to their little bunny hearts' content. However, my parents did not raise a quitter, so we pressed on. Thankfully, because the Google Fiber line should have been buried deeper, they didn't hold us financially responsible for the repair. And graciously, this was only the line running directly to our house, not the entire surrounding neighborhood. I mean, do we really need one more reason for the neighbors to not be excited about this project?

By the end of the weekend, the fence was up. I told the plant babies to breathe a breath of fresh air. They were safe. The bunnies wouldn't be a problem anymore.

Just kidding. The bunnies were, in fact, *still* a problem. Even I was not surprised at this point.

Apparently, when the little furry jerks realized there was now a fence blocking their way, they also were not quitters. They decided instead to send their kids into my garden (aka the bunny salad bar) because while the adults could no longer fit inside the 2" by 3" fence openings, the babies sure could. While I can definitely admire the creative thinking here, and for as much as baby bunnies are even cuter than big bunnies, I wanted them *ooouuuttt*.

We decided the best solution would be to zip tie a layer of chicken wire to the bottom of our three-foot-tall fence the following weekend. Jeremy and I were fairly annoyed to have yet *another* project, seeing as the flowers were still. not. growing. We also dug ourselves another

$80 in the hole because we weren't just going to use silver chicken wire with our black wire metal fence. We're not animals! No, we special ordered black chicken wire online to keep with the suburban aesthetic. I'm proud to share that it ended up working. Pro-tip: Should you ever find yourself in a similar situation, heed my advice and double up on that fencing from the start. Bunnies are savages.

Let's just say a *few* things became painfully obvious. Because naturally, I was just trying to grow some flowers, and ended up growing as a person, too. Rude.

First: Always, and I do mean *always*, "C-A-L-L-B-4-U-[line drawing of a shovel]."

As much as I love to live by "ask forgiveness, not permission," I've learned (ahem—*the hard way*) that caution isn't the enemy of creativity. Wisdom and spontaneity aren't opposites—they're dance partners. There's a reason the saying is "Ready, Set, Go." This flower garden? Total "Go, Ready, Set" energy. Now, renting a power auger to dig a three-foot hole? That definitely needed to be "Ready, Set, *maybe double check*, Go."

A well-placed pause won't ruin the party. Wisdom and caution can usually serve us well—not to kill the vibe, but to protect what we're building. Taking a breath between "go" and "grow" is where clarity can rise, where intuition whispers, and where God might gently redirect your steps before you dig too deep. Slowing down doesn't mean you're losing momentum. It oftentimes means you're paying attention.

Second: Boundaries matter.

As silly as it sounds, that fence wasn't just about keeping bunnies out—it was about protecting what I was trying to grow. Those little fluffballs had *plenty* of yard to snack on. They didn't also need access to the most tender, intentional part of it. And honestly? A lot of people don't need access to the most tender parts of my heart, either.

Boundaries are not mean, selfish, or cold. They are kind, necessary, and, honestly, a sign of maturity I wish I'd figured out sooner.

I've always been wired to care deeply and give freely. But I've also blurred lines, overcommitted, and convinced myself that being available to everyone meant I was being loving. The truth? Constant availability isn't the same thing as love—it's often just exhaustion in disguise.

Boundaries have helped me protect not only my energy, but also my purpose. They've also helped me see which relationships in my life are reciprocal and which ones just want to nibble at my edges. The truth is, some people are only comfortable with you when you're available, agreeable, and asking nothing in return. But genuine relationships— the healthy, life-giving kind—don't flinch when you draw a line. They honor it. They're still there when the gate closes for a minute. They don't need constant access to know you care.

I'm still learning. Still adjusting. Still zip-tying emotional chicken wire where needed. Because here's the deal: If someone gets offended when you build a fence, they were probably planning to snack on something that wasn't theirs to begin with.

Even beautiful things need fences.
Especially the ones still trying to grow.

CHAPTER SEVEN

THE PEACE YOU PLANT

This wasn't our first "all in" moment, not by a long shot. A few years before the cut flower garden, during the pandemic, Jeremy and I bought the cutest little A-frame cabin in the woods with dreams of turning it into a wildly successful short-term rental. Because obviously that's what you do during a global crisis.

It all started in the late summer of 2020, when the school district announced our boys wouldn't be returning to in-person school for a while. After several months of pandemic lockdown, the walls of our house seemed to be closing in on us, so I thought a change of scenery would be good for everyone. I went full detective-mode on every rental site I could find, hunting specifically for a dog-friendly, air-conditioned cabin within two to four hours of home—bonus points if it was on water.

That's when I stumbled upon a place called Innsbrook Resort tucked just outside the west end of St. Louis. It had dozens of rentable A-frames—some on water, some in the woods—and somehow, despite living only three hours away my whole life, I had never heard of it. It was perfect for what we needed, so we booked a four-night stay the following week.

I still remember the stars. Innsbrook is just far enough outside the city that the skies get really dark, and because of their genius light and noise regulations, it felt like we were staying in an open-air planetarium. Our rental had a canoe and a couple of kayaks we used during the day, but the *real* magic—at least for me—was paddling out at night. We would go out on the pond right behind the cabin and float around, listening to the night sounds of bugs and frogs with the light from the surrounding cabins glowing like lanterns and reflecting in the water. Above us, a canopy of stars twinkled in the night sky. It felt like my soul exhaled under those stars after several scary months of navigating everything Covid required of us, and I was grateful.

It was maybe that third day we were there when Jeremy and I bravely started dreaming of what potentially owning an A-frame cabin one day, specifically at Innsbrook, might be like. Though it felt like one of those wild, audacious dreams you say out loud and then quickly start thinking through how unrealistic it is, circumstances changed the following year, and we were able to put a down payment on a place of our own. Jeremy and I drove out almost every weekend for six months straight, renovating the place from top to bottom. Using the phrase "1970s swagger with a hint of Wes Anderson" as our design aesthetic guide, we transformed the place little by little and are still to this day more proud of that place than we are of many projects in which we have invested our time. We named it *The Cocoon Chalet* because that's exactly what it became for us: cozy and transformative.

I remember Jeremy telling me once as we drove through the main entrance of Innsbrook, "I can feel my blood pressure lower when we drive through that gate." I couldn't have agreed more. One of my favorite things to do with him while we visit is watch the sunset over Lake Aspen. We head to our secret spot, typically with a bottle of wine and a couple of glasses, and sip slowly as we watch the light shift and the lake ripple in, fish occasionally jumping nearby. One of us always seems to say mid-sunset, "We really should come here more often."

Innsbrook also unexpectedly awakened in us a love and appreciation of birds. When we spend time outside at our cabin, we typically pull out one of our phones and open up our bird song identification app, *Merlin Bird ID*. Yes, as a matter of fact, we do have a bird app on our phones—let me live my life. We set a phone on the patio table with the app running and let it tell us what birds it detects singing their unique songs around us. Check this: We've become people who can now sometimes pick out what bird is singing even *without* the app. Impressive, I know. And yes, I'm literally bragging about how familiar I am with bird songs. I am aware.

For those of you who are perhaps unfamiliar with this kind of goodness, let me tell you—it is peace at its finest. To zone in on nothing but the faintest songs being sung around you is a version of meditation I can truly get behind. It heightens your sense of awareness and hones your skill of noticing. It's like somewhere along the line I learned to tune the radio dial (remember those?) ever so slightly to pick up on this subtle life frequency, and now that I've found it, I want to protect it at all costs.

I remember a night Jeremy and I were sitting outside at the cabin listening to birds long enough for the sun to set. As the day shifted to night, so did the sounds. Did you know an entire chorus of nature's night sounds starts right as its day sounds end? It's not an abrupt stop and start, either. It's an ever-so-subtle blending of the two that is truly incredible.

We've now listened to the transition more times than I can count, and every time it happens, I picture an orchestra conductor motioning like they do with a symphony for the string section to quiet and the wind section to take the lead. It's glorious to be that un-busy, to intentionally choose to quiet all the noise of life and listen to nature instead. This is why Jeremy says going to stay at our cabin lowers his blood pressure, and this is why we always wish we had more time there.

Gardening has become my opportunity to practice this kind of awareness daily at home. To quiet the noise of life and tune that radio dial ever so slightly to pick up on this new life frequency. I love the sound of bees buzzing around me as they feast on the blossoms I'm tending. I can't get enough of watching butterflies land on flowers nearby, their wings opening and closing at rhythms you can never predict. I can even pick out many of the bird songs that surround me in my neighborhood—ones I learned while being at our cabin.

Can I also hear the sound of cars passing by, bats swinging and cracking against baseballs at the high school across the street, and lawn mowers in my neighborhood every now and again? Sure. It's all part of the symphony of a suburb. But as I breathe in and breathe out, snipping that day's harvest of blooms, I also find my blood pressure regulates. I focus on the color variations of zinnia petals and the details of how assorted dahlias break forth, daily becoming more and more layered and beautiful. I watch the white corn cockle flutter in the breeze and touch the silvery rose strawflower, always mesmerized by its unique texture.

Gardening teaches me to notice. To breathe. To slow down enough to remember what's really important. To focus on beauty instead of fixating so much on the hard things of the world that I will never be able to fix. It becomes an escape where I can recenter and recharge without ever having to pack a bag and leave town. It becomes a sanctuary to experience the Divine in new and incredible ways I would never experience anywhere else.

I will gladly stand out in my garden and enter into the peace it gives me because I've learned how essential that kind of peace is. The rhythms of nature remind us we're not machines. We need rest and joy and beauty like we need air and water and food. When I go outside, I listen to the fish crow overhead, the cardinal in the tree nearby, and the song sparrow somewhere in the distance. I pull the most delicate apricot China Aster into my hand and study its layers of petals glowing almost yellow from the center. As the Bells of Ireland blow in the wind, I imagine them actually ringing. (I mean, wouldn't that be amazing?) I celebrate as the seeds of the purple basil I planted start to form their second layer of leaves as they pop out of the ground, so dark they're almost camouflaged by the soil below. And without even thinking about it, I find myself breathing deeper and slower, becoming centered, finding contentment, and discovering peace amongst the chaos. It's almost, one could say, like I'm on vacation.

Peace doesn't always just find us—we often have to make it. We carve it out and protect it, the same way we tend a little garden plot or guard a weekend away. The real work of becoming isn't about hustling harder or fixing everything that's broken. It's about learning to center yourself in the middle of a noisy, distracted world. To tune the dial. To notice the songbirds. To celebrate the smallest signs of life. Perhaps the most profound thing we can do is slow down long enough to say, *"This is good. Right here. Right now."*

Because peace isn't always somewhere else. It isn't a faraway cabin in the woods or a luxury you earn once everything else is done. Sometimes it's as close as your own backyard—as close as a zinnia blooming in the morning light or a robin's song you've finally learned to hear.

Sometimes, peace is a place you build—and then you go out and stand in it barefoot, coffee in hand, and you stay awhile.

You listen.
You breathe.
You remember who you are.

And in that quiet, rooted space—just like in our beloved *Cocoon Chalet*—you transform.

CHAPTER EIGHT

THE WAIT WAS WORTH IT

Before I got married, I held what many suggested to be "unrealistic expectations." I readily admit I left just about every first date with a reason I knew it would never work. I'd check in with friends after meeting someone new, and they'd almost expect it—*the reason*.

"He had tassels on his loafers."

"He crossed his arms super weird, like Mary Katherine Gallagher on *Saturday Night Live*."

"He ordered four pastries at Starbucks and *then* asked for extra caramel in his caramel Frappuccino."

I'll be the first to admit there was *always* something, whether it was warranted or, occasionally, pretty ridiculous. It used to drive my dad crazy more than anyone. I remember him telling me multiple times, "You should at least give him a chance, Kelly." Maybe so, but I'm convinced it worked out exactly as it should.

On Sunday, October 21, 2012, I walked into a local coffee shop to meet Jeremy for the first time. When he turned around to greet me,

I knew he was different almost immediately. I felt it in my bones. I was so quickly taken with him in person, I'm almost sure I audibly gasped as I felt a near magnetic pull towards him. (Though I sure did try to play it cool. See also: next paragraph.) If you had asked me before that date if I believed in love at first sight, I would have laughed. No freaking way did I think it was real. And maybe it wasn't *love* I necessarily developed in those first few seconds of seeing him, but something incredibly significant certainly started for me that day.

I went up to offer a warm hello, and somehow said instead, "You sure look a lot like my brother-in-law!"

Talk about eight words I wish I could have sucked back in my mouth the second they left.

"Well, that can't be good," Jeremy replied.

I then tried to assure him that Nate is indeed an attractive guy, but heard the actual words coming out of my mouth as I combined "brother-in-law" with "attractive" and tried quickly to correct myself by saying something else equally as asinine.

"JUST! STOP! TALKING!!" I shouted to myself silently.

I should have simply turned around and exited the building—trying a redo upon a playful and lighthearted reentry, signifying I knew how terribly I had started things.

"What's good here?" Jeremy said, graciously pivoting the conversation to the menu and saving me from myself.

Our coffees were served in One More Cup's iconic yellow mugs, and two hours slipped by in a blur of laughter and effortless conversation. I am thrilled to report he did not order extra caramel, or even a Frappuccino. I was instantly smitten—basically one simple coffee away from writing his name in cursive on my notebook. I was a goner, and I knew it.

I remember leaving that date thinking I would be devastated if I didn't get to see him again. This was completely new territory for me. When

I got to my car, I called my friend Jeff, letting him know I wasn't dead in the woods somewhere (online dating requires this kind of thing).

"How was it? What's wrong with this guy?" he asked.

"Nothing. I actually really like him," I replied.

I'm pretty sure Jeff's response was, "Uh oh."

Thirteen months later, we were married. It was the easiest and most certain decision I have ever made in my life. Being with Jeremy has always felt like home, and our connection is more than I could have ever asked for or imagined. We believe the best about each other, have one another's backs, cheer each other on to be the greatest versions of ourselves, love traveling the world together, design beautiful spaces together, and make each other laugh until our sides hurt. There is no one I'd rather have by my side in all things, and I pray regularly we will have more years together than I had on my own.

It's the little things with Jeremy, however, that make life so incredible. Top of that list recently has been our daily garden walk. Every night after work, the first thing we do is go outside and stroll around the garden bed, looking for what little gifts might be waiting for us. We'll point out to each other little buds starting on the buttercream stock or the next bloom opening on the chantilly bronze snapdragons. We'll troubleshoot why the sweet peas aren't flowering yet, and discuss possible solutions we've found online. We'll admire the latest zinnia and the tired little bumblebee sleeping on it.

It's my absolute favorite thing knowing he cares so much about the details, and my joy in this process is made more complete because of his presence and excitement for everything. Would I still love doing it on my own? Of course, but there is something deeply wonderful about having someone so invested in the process with whom you always get to share it. I have likened it to putting an exclamation point at the end of a sentence versus a period. My mom—who I have often called my human exclamation point—had a way of doing this better than anyone, but Jeremy is definitely a very close second.

I'm convinced God brought both Jeremy and gardening into my life so that I could learn to calm the freak down a little better. Chill is basically Jeremy's middle name, seeing as he's easily the most relaxed person I know. It's one of his best—and most annoying—qualities.

The number of times I have heard him say "I'm not worried about it" is nothing short of enraging, but that's clearly not a defect in him. It's more a reflection of my need to control things that are not mine to control, especially in regards to time. I tend to stress when I don't think there is "enough time", things are taking "too much time", or things haven't started "on time". I have a lot to learn from Jeremy's laissez-faire approach to life, but maybe I needed another teacher, and that's why gardening found me.

Gardening will teach you nothing if not patience. If you're not yet in the garden club, it takes an average of 60-120 days for a seed to become a flower—and that's assuming you've done everything right to help it germinate in the first place. I've already detailed all the missteps I had to this point, so let's just say that having a hand to hold was precisely what I needed when we first got things planted and would walk out to the garden every day, hoping my seedlings hadn't shriveled up and died. It all felt so fragile—so out of my control. But this process has reinforced for me how true it is that good things come to those who wait. I literally jump up and down when I see something start to bloom. It is unreal the level of joy and fulfillment a little bud can bring after weeks of giving it tender loving care.

I have been horribly impatient most of my life. Like, embarrassingly so. As a result, I have an uncanny ability to choose the slowest line at any store and hit every red light while driving, especially when I am running late. Impatient people are always hyper aware of how dreadfully long those situations take. Their (ok … my) blood pressure escalates with every blessed minute that something's taking longer than expected. And if someone even suggests that they "need to be more patient," watch out. Them's fightin' words. Though they might be true, they are never helpful to hear in a moment when patience has left the building and irrational rage has taken over.

Meeting Jeremy and knowing wholeheartedly that the wait for him was not only worthwhile but for a reason, honestly, mellowed me out *a ton*. Hindsight is such a gift. I swear to you, though, my garden helps me develop patience more than anything—perhaps even hindsight. It teaches me quite literally that everything beautiful takes time to become so. That growth is a process that requires an uncertain amount of time, which, coincidentally, is also not completely ours to dictate.

While we have Instagram and TikTok to thank for giving most of humanity the attention span of eight whopping seconds, while I'm in my garden I can somehow manage to completely lose track of time staring at butterflies fluttering about my zinnia patch and bees feasting on the celosia plumes. I can spend days enjoying each and every stage an individual blossom goes through as it breaks from bud to full bloom, and I can relish little details like how the breeze feels against my skin on a hot day after hours of pulling weeds.

Time kind of stands still for me when I'm gardening. I enter Jeremy-level chill zones when I'm in my garden, and I smile, knowing how good it is for me to be this relaxed. Being this connected to nature allows me to exhale at a soul level. I don't worry about how productive I'm being. I'm just … being. When I'm in my garden, I'm quiet, reflective, aware, and grateful at levels nothing else will bring out in me. In the garden, I feel like my best self. When I leave, filled up with its beauty and goodness, I carry it all with me into the regular rhythms of life— the ones that don't always bring out my best. Sometimes (not always, but sometimes) that beauty steadies me, softens me, and helps me relax just a bit more than I normally would.

Turns out both love and beauty take their sweet time. Often, they arrive when we've learned to wait with open hands. When we've figured out how to trade anxiety for hope and worry for wonder. They show up when they're ready. Because the best things—the ones truly worth having—rarely ever show up on our timeline.

CHAPTER NINE

THE BEETLE BROTHEL

Japanese beetles are bastards.

I said what I said.

I am truly convinced they are proof that hell exists, and you simply will not be able to convince me otherwise.

I remember the first time I saw them years ago, before I really got into gardening. A couple of them had found their way inside our home, and other than wishing they were outside, as I wish all bugs would remain, I honestly thought they were beautiful. The way their metallic-looking shells glimmered iridescently was magical to me. In fact, I thought they were so special I would pick them up and bring them safely back outside, like I was rescuing living gemstones or something. And this is saying a lot, because I usually leave bug duty to Jeremy. When I later learned how utterly destructive they can be, I wished I had flushed them when I had the chance.

That first spring in the garden, after working so hard to water and care for my seedlings—nurturing them weekly with the stinky liquid fish guts and carefully weeding around them as they rooted deep—

these jerk wads had the nerve to find my beloved zinnia patch and start feasting on them with a fervor that paled the work of the baby bunnies. I didn't know what to do, just as I hadn't known anything along the way since starting my cut flower garden. So I did what most people knew to do in the year of our Lord 2023: I searched Google.

I swear I would not have made it in the olden days of yore as a gardener—as in, before the World Wide Web existed. I am officially old enough to know what life was like before WiFi, smartphones, and social media—and there's something inherently wonderful about it all. But for as much as I wholeheartedly believe that, would someone please explain to me how anyone knew what to do about Japanese beetles before the internet? Were there books or microfiche available on them? Would people have to go to their local library and read entire books about gardening to figure out what was going on? As if there is time once they appear in your garden! They can annihilate a patch of flowers in days, and I'm (sadly) a very slow reader. I'm honestly perplexed about this.

Here I was in my first year of gardening, watching my zinnia leaves become so hole-y they looked crocheted, and all I had to do was type into my iPhone "why are there so many holes in my zinnia leaves" to have a photo of a Japanese beetle pop up as the expected culprit. I'm pretty certain under said photo read the caption "these jerks are to blame."

Thankfully, Google also quickly gave me a handful of ways to address this issue. The first method involved picking them off by hand and putting them in a bucket of soapy water, which prevented them from flying back out. So barbaric, right? Talk about a slow and painful death, but I did as I was told. Every day, I would go out with said bucket of soapy water, looking for these boogers and throwing as many of them in as I could find. Awkwardly...there were so many who were oftentimes coupled up and found <ahem> "making beetle babies" with one another, I jokingly started referring to my cut flower garden as a Japanese Beetle Brothel. It was so prolific I wondered if I should start playing some Marvin Gaye for them or perhaps offer them some teeny-weeny, beetle-sized cigarettes, but I refused to encourage the activity. There was no denying it—my garden was infested. It's like they had all gotten the memo that a new gardener was in town and the party was at Kelly's house.

I tried everything, even to the point of putting beer in a bowl and leaving it slightly nestled into the soil. No luck. FYI, Japanese beetles apparently don't like Modelo—spread the word. I put some of the ultra-sticky yellow tape along the fence. Nope. They didn't go for that either. I also put up a trap with the bag and the super fragrant lure which worked for some of them, but then I heard that those traps only draw more to your yard, so I immediately removed them and went back to soapy water. My best defense was to indeed pick them all off by hand. I eventually got ahead of them, or they got to the point in the summer when they start laying eggs in your yard (gross)—but only in time for the next issue to present itself. I swear, if it's not one thing, it's the next when you're gardening. But also in general when you're learning anything new, I'm sure.

For a couple of weeks, I did my fair share of reading about Japanese beetles and learned a few really interesting things. Like, after a leaf has been turned to lace from all the holes being created after their feast, the leaves start to emit odors that actually attract other beetles—like sharks to blood. So though I joke about a memo being sent out about the party being at my house, the garden was actually sending its own form of scented smoke signals to surrounding beetles, declaring the buffet was open. And though you might think it's funny that I was calling it a beetle brothel, virgin female beetles literally produce a pheromone (which I choose to refer to as their "milkshake") that indeed brings all the boys to the yard. Y'all...I know far too much about the reproductive life of Japanese beetles at this point, but 'tis what happens when you're a gardener with Google.

I readied myself for year two. There's a milk spore something-or-other I read about that apparently might help, and I looked into companion planting. Talk about Gardening 2.0! Yet I also know there is nothing more effective than throwing them into a bucket of soapy water. Simple enough, if you just make a point of doing it a couple of times a day. Furthermore, I know they're easier to catch in the cool air of the morning when they're less active, so I'll be starting my days beetle hunting. And this is my life now—setting an alarm to meet the groggy spawns of Satan as they wake, all in hopes of preserving my flower babies and giving them every fighting chance they can get.

I laugh now as I remember my initial impression of Japanese beetles. Those shiny metallic shells were so deceptively gorgeous, I honestly thought I was doing the world a favor by saving them. I now stand on the side of having experienced firsthand how quick, thorough, and merciless their destruction can be, and I know better.

I've been tricked more than once by shiny objects in life—everything from wanting to be friends with certain people, the hope of quick and easy money, the insatiable craving for more than I can afford … just to name a few. Sometimes the sheer lure of shiny is enough to take your eyes off what's right in front of you and birth discontentment—and that discontentment can surely breed its own form of bitterness.

As I grow older, I'm learning to proceed with caution when it comes to anything too alluring. Shiny has a sneaky way of biting you in the bootay. Let it take too many chomps and you'll find your badonkadonk metaphorically looking a lot like my zinnia leaves when you least expect it.

The danger with shiny things is how quickly they can cause demise—oftentimes before you even see it coming. Destruction rarely announces itself; sometimes it simply glimmers. You almost have to expect it and prepare for it to happen. So my suggestion? Always have one eye open, appreciating the beauty in front of you, and the other keeping watch for anything that could destroy it.

Just make sure to be discerning. It might be shiny and pretty, but it might also be the devil in disguise. If it's a Japanese Beetle eating your flowers, I'm convinced it is.

CHAPTER TEN

ALONG CAME A SUPPORT SYSTEM

I'm still flabbergasted that my cut flower garden ever managed to produce a single bud that first year. Yet, I stand by what I shared earlier: nature doesn't just want to survive—it wants to grow. Sometimes so much that it takes yanking a plant out by the roots before it finally gets the message that it's not welcome. I've watched flowers in my garden start off so weak, they'd topple over from the weight of their own heads. But they didn't quit. Some of them would literally grow sideways across the soil, inching along the surface until they built up enough strength to lift themselves and start growing upright again. It was fascinating—and honestly, pretty dang inspiring. Their will to live was so relentless, it made me stop and ask myself: *How hard am I willing to work for my own blooming?*

That first summer, once my flowers finally started to take off in the compost that resembled mulch, I saw more and more of them toppling over and realized something needed to be done. Google came to the rescue once again, and in less than two minutes, I learned I needed to purchase some support netting, so off to Menards we went (again) to snag some.

When we arrived, there was an entire row of things in the garden center I'd never had to shop for before. Though we had come for support netting, the cart quickly started filling with a bunch of other things it seemed we needed as well: Posts for the netting. Some more posts for the dahlias soon. And, of course, some ties to bind the dahlia stalks to said posts. You might assume gardening is an inexpensive hobby. How much can it cost to just "buy some seeds and plant them in the ground"? Friend, I'm here to let you in on the truth about gardening. I could write quite the sequel to *If You Give a Mouse a Cookie* based on all we had to invest that first year in getting this garden to take off. And yet we'd come this far. Were we really not going to buy the support gear at this point? Nosireeebobski. Pass the Mastercard, please.

When we got home, Jeremy and I began the work of getting the netting over the zinnias. It was clear within seconds how much easier it would have been to put this out right as they were planted. (Note to self: Do that next time.) It probably would also have been easier to install if our garden were laid out in clean rows, as most flower farmers use with clear margins on each side. But I, again, always tend to do things the hard way.

We weren't on an acreage. We were in the 'burbs. So, clearly, we used the only space in our yard with the right kind of light, and in wanting to maximize every square inch available to us, we quite literally created a triangle-shaped garden bed. I mean … why wouldn't we have? Seems logical, since I've never seen a triangle-shaped garden bed before. Also, it wasn't planted in rows. Instead, I had little pockets of flower varieties here and there with very little order. It made sense to me when I looked at it on paper—and I loved how organic it all grew. But because of this, Jeremy and I had the privilege of trying to cut support netting into various sizes that covered these obscure zones and then attempt to use the posts to hold them in place, all while walking in and around these incredibly tenacious zinnias growing along the ground and then up again, sprawling far beyond the space they use when they grow "normally."

If I had been my own neighbor last summer, I would have popped some popcorn and stood by the window watching this all go down, laughing hysterically. *"What are they up to now?"* has got to be a question more than one of them asked as they saw us working in this garden, but especially as we manhandled the support netting trying to get it in place.

Ever tried covering a casserole dish with cheap plastic wrap? It sticks to itself—check. Clumps up and won't stay where you put it—check. Turns into way more drama than necessary—double check. Now multiply that mess by a thousand, and you've basically lived through our late-season support netting install.

Wouldn't you know, though, after all was said and done, growth became next level in the garden. The flowers that had been struggling all of a sudden straightened up and grew as they were intended. When strong winds would come with summer storms, I no longer worried about them. I knew they were going to be just fine. You could almost audibly hear the flowers themselves exhale as they relaxed into the support offered them.

I know full well I have personally experienced growth without the necessary support system in place. Though growth can happen, it's often messy and not very direct. When I have the people and things in place around me, guiding me and cheering me on as I stretch myself to take new steps, I thrive in ways I simply could not on my own.

For example, the same summer I planted my cut flower garden for the first time, I simultaneously joined the gym around the corner and committed to getting healthier. We had a treadmill and a Peloton in the basement, but out of nowhere, I started feeling a nudge to return to the pool.

When I was growing up, my parents did a great job of encouraging me and my sisters to be active by doing little things like "forcing" us (well, at least me) to swim on the neighborhood summer swim team. Lord knows I wouldn't have chosen to do it on my own, especially in high school. Waking up at o'dark thirty for daily swim practice was *not* my idea of a good time. Instead, I preferred staying up late and sleeping in, but there would be none of that in the Jackson household. I cannot count the number of times I heard my dad say, "You can't soar with the eagles in the morning if you hoot with the owls at night." To which I always wanted to say, "But what if the owls are more fun?"

Though I resented my parents for it back in high school, getting back in the pool felt like a homecoming of sorts.

I remember those first times back in the pool—the extraordinary sensation of gliding through the water, the rhythm of strokes and kicks returning like old friends. It felt like alignment, like something inside me had finally clicked into place. Almost instantly, I realized what a gift my parents had given me by insisting on swim team all those years ago, and I felt nothing but gratitude.

After a few days, I realized I'd have to push past the usual suspects—soreness, boredom, and plain old laziness—if I was going to keep up with my plan of swimming multiple times a week. So, I got strategic. I bought bone conduction headphones so I could blast 1990s rap and hip hop while I swam (Dr. Dre and Eminem deserve serious credit for keeping me moving). I also struck a deal with myself: Finish the workout, and I earned ten glorious minutes in the hot tub; quit early, and no bubbles for me. But the best move I made was checking out the water aerobics schedule, figuring I could break up the monotony of lap swimming with the occasional group class.

I'd seen the ladies in water aerobics while I swam, their laughter carrying across the pool every time I came up for air. My mom loved water aerobics, too. She adored the classes, but even more so, she adored the women with whom she worked out. Since losing her to pancreatic cancer in 2014, I've grabbed onto any thread of connection I can, and this felt like one of them. My only hesitation before starting was whether I'd get a hard enough workout.

Enter Sarrisa.

I'd been to a couple of water aerobics classes before hers and had already decided aquatic ankle weights were a necessity if I wanted a hard workout. During my first class with Sarrisa, however, having them velcroed in place before she arrived, she waited until *after* class—the very one I struggled to keep up with—to casually say as I was removing them, "Yeah … you don't need those when I'm teaching."

Sarrisa has quickly become one of my favorite humans. She's smart, kind, and runs an incredible nonprofit for people living with Parkinson's. She also walks into the natatorium looking like she could completely kick your ass, coffee in hand. She's built a career helping people care for themselves, toeing the line perfectly between gentle support and "don't mess with me" authority. Even during that first class, I appreciated the fact that she both let me try keeping up with my weights on *and* enjoyed watching me regret my decision to wear them through most of the class.

I decided from that first workout with her that I would go to her class twice a week, breaking up the tedium of lap swimming enough to keep me going. And so began my love affair with water aerobics, with Sarrisa at the helm. I started making friends in class with women 20+ years older than me who cheered me on and always made me laugh. I felt freedom in my body again—something I hadn't felt since my neurologist banned me from lifting more than ten pounds and chronic nerve pain took hold.

The stronger I got, the more often I heard myself say "I can" instead of "I can't." It pushed me even on my lap swimming days to do the same. I started doing speed drills and long swims, choosing one day to spontaneously go from swimming one mile to two just because I wanted to see if I could do it. When I could, I started working towards three. I have never been more committed to exercise since discovering an activity I love to do. Once my brain associated pleasure with swimming, I started to wake up before my alarm, excited to get there.

The pool was changing more than my health—it was reshaping the way I thought about myself. Personal growth, I've learned, is often stunted by belief. When it comes down to it, mindset is everything. I owe so much to Sarrisa and the water aerobics ladies for helping me stay the course that summer. They became my rods and netting, supporting me as I stepped into a new path of growth toward health. Even on days when I was lap swimming during their classes, they'd walk by and cheer me on, telling me how proud they were of my commitment.

I felt seen, supported, and honestly like my mom would have adored them for filling that gap in her absence.

I knew I wanted to grow, but I also knew I couldn't do it alone. I needed the right people and the right tools to keep me going—and I'm so glad I found them before quitting ever crossed my mind. With bone-conduction headphones blasting Lil Jon ("Let's go! If you want it, you can get it"), a water aerobics instructor determined to push every athlete, and a crew of women cheering me on—wouldn't you know? I did.

Support makes growth not just possible—it makes it sustainable. It keeps you upright when the winds pick up and the ground feels shaky. Whether it's floral netting or the right playlist in your headphones, a cheering section of wise women with pool noodles, or someone simply showing up because they believe in you—these are the things that help us bloom.

Build the net.
Fill the lane.
Find your people.

Because sure, you *could* try to grow without it. But why on earth would you want to?

CHAPTER ELEVEN

THE SPACE THAT FOLLOWS

My first year as a cut flower gardener was basically a crash course in timing—and in letting go. Some seeds shot up like overachievers. Others took their sweet time, testing my patience. While some seeds take 60 days to bloom, others take twice as long. I realized, as it all played out in real time, how intentional you must be in the planning process if you want a collection of flowers to bloom simultaneously. Since I hadn't really paid much attention to this when I got started, very little was ready to harvest collectively as I hoped.

I also learned how a few flowers found their sweet spot in the heat, while others fainted the minute summer showed up. Just when I thought I had things figured out, something would wither, leaving me muttering, *"Well, that was rude."*

Failure is often just opportunity showing up in a way you wouldn't have chosen. You have to set your mind to see it that way, but it's true. It gives you the chance to learn, adapt, and stay resilient. It stretches your creative thinking skills and forces you to problem solve. It even invites you to reflect on your commitment to something, giving you the chance to quietly exit stage left—or to realize how deeply rooted your passion is and double down on making it work. For me, all of this failure only revealed how much I loved flowers and how fiercely I wanted to see my garden thrive. So I wrote down what I learned and committed to coming back the next year with a little more intention.

Gardening is basically agreeing to dance with Mother Nature—and that girl not only always leads, she has a knack for stepping on your toes in ways you never see coming. Gardeners don't get to decide how much rain or heat a flower needs—or what it'll actually get in a given season. You can only adjust so much to whatever she doles out. Add in your own human error, and it's basically a match made in Weirdosville. Case in point: I have an uncanny ability to sow seeds right before a flash flood, only to watch everything wash away. Sure, I could go hunting for them, but that feels rather futile. More often than not, the best option is to start over—or to plant something entirely new in its place.

Still, nothing drove this lesson home more than my experience with dahlias—the drama queens of the garden. They play by a set of rules that feel both wildly particular and totally outside my control. Dahlias tend to shine in September in my part of the country. Though I've seen some local flower farmers get them earlier, it's from a mix of accumulated knowledge and having the right conditions—most of which are still out of their control despite how much they know. For the rest of us, we plant dahlia tubers after the last frost and hope for the best. Too much cold, soggy soil, and the tubers will throw a tantrum and rot underground—like they'd rather die theatrically than endure less-than-perfect conditions.

It's just another dance with the always leading lady, Mother Nature. She changes the song halfway through and dares you to keep up. Sometimes it works out, and sometimes it doesn't. You can't exactly prevent a heatwave. You also can't make flowers un-wilt. While there's always room to adapt and improve, I'm learning to let everything have its season—and to accept that I have little to no control over what that season will be.

As a person of faith, I've heard the verse, "There is a time for everything, and a season for every activity under the heavens," probably 800,000 times (give or take a few). It's shared at funerals often because of the words that come next—"a time to be born and a time to die." But it's the stanza after that—"a time to plant and a time to uproot"—that has become so meaningful to me. (Ecclesiastes 3:1-2, NIV)

I understood it before, but now I really *get* it. I've seen that reality unfold in countless ways since I started this garden. I find myself quoting it when I don't like what's happening, whether I can change it or not. As much as I want snapdragons to thrive in the heat of the summer, most of them prefer cooler weather. I can wish all day for that to change, or I can celebrate them while they bloom and turn my attention to what's next in line to shine. It doesn't do me one bit of good—or change the outcome whatsoever—to wish for something different. If I'm so focused on being sad about snapdragons being past their prime, am I even ready to help usher the next variety into bloom?

Sometimes, when a plant has outgrown its space and overcrowds the rest, I just have to make the call. I can either fight the reality of it and likely end up with a fungus infestation due to a lack of airflow, ultimately destroying the entire crop, or I can do the hard thing and rip out what's taking up too much room. Uprooting is hard. It's really sad to rip out plants that have grown this much and hung in there this long. But I'd choose it every time over letting everything rot because I was unwilling to do the hard thing. Uprooting takes wisdom, awareness, courage, a vision for what's next—and yes, even appreciation for what was. It can feel harsh, but often, it's the kindest thing you can do. It's the clearest sign that one thing's time has ended, and another's time is on its way.

Hardwired into each seed sown are conditions to which they are intended to respond. Germination happens at a certain temperature. Seedlings need a specific number of hours in the sun each day to grow to their full potential. Plants know the season in which they are intended to bloom, and though it seems like they're taking their sweet time, it is all on schedule.

There is a beautiful surrender in realizing you can't change any of it. Even down to the fact that in each specific area of the world, due to its unique climate, there is a time to harvest. And after harvest, a time for rest. Lord knows the Earth and I both need it after a full (hot) summer in the garden.

This reality of seasonality teaches such an important life lesson, one I have experienced most significantly in friendships. The first thing that comes to mind is one of my favorite photos from our wedding day in 2013. We had a small-ish ceremony and chose not to have a wedding party stand with us, mainly because we wanted it to be hyper-focused on the commitment Jeremy and I were making not only to each other but also to his two boys, David and JJ. And, well … I was 38. Picking bridesmaids felt impossible. That's a lot of life lived and a lot of meaningful friendships made.

Instead, we asked everyone in attendance to walk down to the altar as they entered the church and light a candle, symbolizing their love and support for us through the years. As a result, we had just over 100 floating candles in various-sized vases lit by the people who'd shaped us. It was the most beautiful backdrop to our ceremony.

Right before the pastor entered with Jeremy and the boys, the four most important friends in my life at the time, who had been with me all day as I was getting ready, walked to the front together. One of our photographers caught this incredible moment where each of them holds an expression so true to who they are. One of them was crying, another was laughing, another was looking at the one crying with an expression oozing with empathy and compassion, and the last was having trouble with the lighter. As a grown woman nearing her 40s, I thought for sure they would be my forever people—the ones I would grow old with and see through thick and thin. Today, however, almost eleven years later, I am in regular contact with only a couple of them. This still astounds me.

There are vast parts of me that grieve the loss of connection with them. I miss so much of who they are and the friendships we shared. There are other parts of me, however, after working through the grief a little, that choose to celebrate the season of life we shared together. I am beyond grateful for the impact we had on one another for a time and the women we helped each other become. I'm also very hopeful our friendships will resurface if time and circumstances allow. However, I've become very aware that friendships—much like jobs, houses, hobbies, flowers in the garden, and all sorts of other things—can be beautiful parts of your life for a season, and then not be … and that's ok. They don't have to be forever to be meaningful.

We rarely get answers to why a friendship faded. If we're honest, even having one doesn't always help. Sometimes there's no fault, no fallout—just a shift … and that's okay, too. Sometimes, as a result of grieving, blessing, and releasing what once was, we ultimately make room for what's next.

There are women in my life now who I can't imagine not knowing. Women who showed up *after* the shifts. Women who have significant, important voices in my life today. They have become my new first calls and reach-out-to's after big life moments. But without the shifts that have taken place, I'm not sure I would have ever thought to make space for them like I have, and I would have missed out on the unique and incredible perspective they bring to my world.

Over time, I've come to believe this: There is raw, redemptive goodness in acknowledging and accepting what's no longer what it was—and choosing to make space for what's ready to be.

There's a time to plant—full of nurture, intention, and hope. But there's also a time to uproot, and honestly, that takes just as much care and just as much guts. So if you need someone to tell you it's okay for something—or someone—to only be in your life for a season, here it is: It's okay. I promise. It really is.

What matters is not letting it turn you bitter. Don't camp out in the grief and uncertainty forever, and for the love, don't beat yourself up with endless "whys." Let the shift be what it is, and hold gratitude for the beauty, the joy, and the lessons it gave you while it lasted—because sometimes that's the whole point.

There truly is a time for everything. We rarely get to choose what that timing is, but we do get to choose how we respond. When something is uprooted, feel the sting—but then make sure to lift your eyes. See the space and imagine what could grow there next.

Plant again, and when it blooms, let it have its season, as well. Maybe it's perennial; maybe it's short-lived. Either way, it will be beautiful and exactly as it's meant to be. Just make sure you don't miss it while mourning what no longer is.

CHAPTER TWELVE

UNAPOLOGETICALLY EXTRA

I readily admit it: I own a Stanley. The 40-ounce tumbler with handle and straw, to be exact.

I'm not one to typically jump on trends—especially ones where women are carrying around cups the size of milk jugs—but my bestie convinced me one warm summer night to try hers while we sat in their backyard. She told me all the reasons she loved it: how long the water stayed cold, how perfectly it fit in her car's cupholder, and something maybe even about how the *girth of the straw* led her to stay "more hydrated" than with any other cup she owned. I raised an eyebrow. Could a cup *really* be superior in hydration potential? I was skeptical. However, because we've been friends for 25 years, I listened, opened my mind to how life-changing this cup might be ... and proceeded to slurp up 40 ounces of water in record time. Cross my heart. Girl Scout's honor. It was shocking how fast and easily it all went down the hatch. Though I hated to be so quickly persuaded, I was unequivocally influenced. I *had* to have one.

This all went down in the summer of 2022, when Stanley tumblers were nowhere to be found in retail stores. Since the company only released them a few times a year, people were reselling them on eBay for twice their retail value. I couldn't believe how hard they were to come by—or how people were collecting them to, I don't know … match their outfits? I found myself mildly annoyed that the search for a Stanley was a) taking so long and b) might cost so much. However, since that first night of being introduced to the cup, feeling the cool, crisp H2O course through my veins, every water bottle in my possession paled in comparison. I was forever ruined. Nothing would ever again satisfy except for a Stanley.

I finally found one, and my love affair with Stanley officially began. Jessi was right: I was more hydrated than I had ever been in my life. I'm not being dramatic here. I *felt* it. I had more energy, my skin looked brighter, I didn't crave caffeine as much, and I was sleeping better. Hydration is no joke—it's genuinely essential for well-being. But honestly, Stanley tumblers should come with a Surgeon General's warning because I swear I developed tennis elbow from hauling it everywhere and constantly lifting it to sip. Has a hydration vessel ever caused tendinitis before? I would laugh if I were joking, but I think it actually did. I wasn't walking miles to the well with a jug on my head, but that 40-ounce beast was taking its toll on my already worn elbow, thanks to 20 years as a professional photographer.

That first summer of my cut flower garden, I watered my plants like it was my new part-time job. Had I done any reading on how much water they truly needed? Of course not. But it was in the 90s most of the summer, and as a result, I was extra thirsty, so surely the flowers were as well, right? At least that was my logic. Since they couldn't lounge in the garden sipping their own little flower-sized Stanleys, I pulled out the hose morning and night and soaked them like my life—and theirs—depended on it. Was I overwatering? Maybe. Too frequently? Probably. But they were already stressed from everything else I'd done to them, so par for the course.

Truth be told, I looked forward to those watering sessions every day. Whether or not it was helping the plants, it was helping *me.* The back-and-forth rhythm of the hose became a visual metronome, guiding me to focus on the simple task in front of me. The sound of water hitting leaves was almost hypnotic. It transported me back to Belize, where Jeremy and I once napped with our bungalow windows open, listening to the rain fall on the rainforest canopy. Every time I watered, I breathed a silent prayer that my plants would keep growing and getting stronger. The blooms had finally started popping, revealing a rainbow of colors and layers of beauty after a long season of being only green. I was bursting at the seams with joy. After so much struggle, my garden was finally thriving! Well, thriving enough for a rookie flower grower to be thrilled. It felt like watching a miracle unfolding, seeing it all come to life after not being sure it would at all.

I've heard it said that to plant flowers is to believe in hope—to engage actively in the building of tomorrow's goodness. You care for them in expectation that something beautiful is coming—but you don't know which of them will survive. I've planted rows of seeds that never germinated, or were stolen by birds before they had a chance. I've planted too early, and I've planted too late. I've overwatered, and I've underwatered. Yet there always was a strong likelihood that, despite all the whoopsiedoodles, something would still grow. It wouldn't all grow, but something would.

That first summer, watering my garden became an act of hope. Maybe that's why it felt so good to start and end my days doing it. Hope is good for the soul, especially in the chaos we all live through. There's so much heaviness and heartache, I get pummeled by it regularly. But then I have these moments in the garden—watching the impossible become possible—and my soul fills with a joy that's more refreshing than ice-cold Stanley water through an extra-wide straw. That kind of joy settles deep. It's an amuse-bouche of the beauty that's still on its way.

That beauty mostly comes from hydration, adequate sunshine, and, in my opinion, the kindness of God. I can't make these things grow on my own. My role is small—placing them in the right kind of light and doing my best to keep them watered. The rest is far beyond my control. Isn't that something to consider? So much of what I try to grip tightly was never mine to manage in the first place. And if a dahlia can unfurl under God's care, then surely the details of my own life are not beyond what the Divine is willing to nurture.

Speaking of dahlias ... want to hear a couple things about what has become my favorite flower?

Dahlias, unlike everything else I grow, don't want much water until they break the surface of the soil. Dig a hole, insert tuber, and then basically leave it the heck alone until it's showing life above ground. Ironically, once they grow a few sets of leaves, they want more water than most everything else I have planted—just not too late at night. Let me be *real* clear about that. NOT. TOO. LATE. AT. NIGHT. They need time for their leaves to dry in the sun, or mildew can set in. Basically, dahlias are proof that the right care at the wrong time is still the wrong move. It might sound a little "extra," but dahlias *are* extra—and worth every bit of TLC they require.

Perhaps my favorite thing about dahlias, however, is how they seem to breathe as they bloom. In a time-lapse video I once saw, you can actually watch them pull inward—like a contraction—before each new layer of petals unfurls. It's a big, bold reminder that growth isn't always outward. Sometimes it's a cycle: inhale, exhale, sip, refill. Just like hydration, growth works best when it comes in steady rhythms.

We aren't meant to produce, expand, or be in bloom constantly. There's goodness in drawing inward, pausing, and resting before we reveal what's next—in allowing growth to move you beyond who you have known yourself to be thus far, extending into a more evolved, complete expression of who you are intended to become. I'm not always good about this, honestly. I prefer to quantify my time, listing off all that I've accomplished as proof that I used my days well. The older I get, however, the more I understand: Rest and reflection aren't indulgent—they're essential—like water breaks for the soul. Skip them, and eventually you'll wilt. Likewise, taking a moment to breathe before giving more of yourself is not only wise—it's requisite. Even the strongest blooms can't thrive without it.

So consider this permission to be more like a dahlia and less like a wildflower. Be as extra as you need to be. Discover what you uniquely require at every stage and turn of growth. And don't you dare apologize for it. Not one bit. Lean into growth. Look forward to what's next. But also? Find time to inhale, rest, reflect, hydrate, and prepare for what is coming. Growth for every person has a custom timeline, and the beauty you will bring as a result is worth everything it takes.

Your beauty will bloom on *your* schedule, in *your* way. Own that truth deeply. Be confident that what it will take to bring your one-of-a-kind, sometimes quirky or eccentric goodness into the world is worth whatever it requires. Just make sure when it's time, you unabashedly let it all shine. Bloom boldly, fully, and unapologetically, because you have something truly worth sharing. Don't hold back—serve it to the world Stanley-sized.

CHAPTER THIRTEEN

THE LONG GOODBYE

There may have been a slight complication born out of my over-eager watering schedule, or maybe it just showed up because it's what tends to happen when autumn sets in around Kansas City. Regardless, I remember the day I went out to my garden and saw little white spots starting to appear on the leaves of my zinnias. I wasn't sure what they were—or, quite honestly, how long they'd even been there. At the time, the blooms still looked incredibly healthy, so I didn't worry too much about it.

When the spots started spreading at what felt like warp speed, I once again turned to Google, my most essential gardening tool. By the time I figured out it was powdery mildew, it was honestly too late to do much about it. A breakout of powdery mildew can wreak havoc fast, sometimes destroying a crop within a week. Since I had no idea when those little white dots had first appeared, the damage was already well underway. You can bet your bottom dollar I'll forever be on the lookout moving forward.

For those who don't know, powdery mildew is a fungal growth that thrives on humidity or—*cue my facepalm*—leaves that don't dry out by the end of the day. Those evening watering sessions I found so meditative and transcendent? The ones that transported me to the Belizean rainforest? Definitely not helpful in this regard. I didn't know powdery mildew was even a thing, let alone how prone zinnias were to this disease, how to prevent it, or how to spot it early enough to hold it at bay. So by the time I understood what was happening, the blooms were showing stress, stalks and leaves were turning a crispy brown, and—because life's a comedy—the mildew had started spreading to the nearby cosmos.

We tried *everything*. Neem oil. Baking soda concoctions. Dish soap and water. I ripped off leaves and prayed the stems and blooms could manage without them. I uprooted the plants that were most severely affected, hoping to spare the rest. Who knows if anything helped at all, but I sure as heck wasn't going to raise a white flag without a fight. We had been fighting for this garden all summer. I wasn't about to go down easy.

We ultimately realized there was nothing that could be done. No matter what we tried, that zinnia patch was showing signs of decay more each day. I felt devastated. Though tears were shed on more than one occasion, I knew it was a waste of energy. I had hoped for a few more weeks of blooms to enjoy before the growing season ended and we let the garden rest for the winter. After all we'd done to get to this point, it just ended so prematurely. It was a hard, hard night when we pulled them out by their roots and shoved them into lawn waste bags, treating them no longer like treasures but like trash.

I read up on powdery mildew (riveting, I know) to figure out how to prevent it next season or how to treat it when it first appears. I reached out to local growers, hoping to hear from people who had walked this flower-growing path and lived to tell the tale. Tired of learning everything the hard way, I wanted the kind of wisdom only heartbreak and experience can teach—as well as the kind of community that reminds you you're not alone.

My approach shifted from just diving in and figuring it out to seeking the kind of knowledge that could guide me through the storm, which always seemed to be brewing in some capacity in my little cut flower bed.

Once we knew what powdery mildew was going to do, we also fully surrendered to pulling out all the cosmos. My precious, delicate cosmos—those soft pink and white blooms that danced high above the rest of the garden like they were doing a slow-motion ballet in the breeze. I had fallen in love with them. Watching them catch the sunlight was literal magic—the kind of backlighting that dreams are made of for a retired photographer. As I uprooted them, I found myself whispering thanks for the gift they had been. I made quiet plans to plant them again the following summer—maybe in different colors? Perhaps some of the double-click varieties? Or maybe the same ones, because honestly, that pink, white, and deep fuchsia combination had been near perfection. I knew I always wanted them somewhere in the garden.

Not long after that, I had to pull up all the dahlias. And one by one, it cut deep. I grieved the loss of their beauty, the joy they had brought me and so many others, and the knowing it would be another nine whole months before I could enjoy this again.

Was it my fault? Could I have prevented this if I had known more? Maybe. Either way, it didn't matter at this point. So I let myself feel the sadness fully and said goodbye to this "Little Garden That Could," which had finally come to life after months of struggle and had brought me such immense delight, beyond anything I expected.

I've learned to recognize grief of any kind or level when it shows up because I've met it many times before. I've faced the unexpected loss of a 20-year career to health issues. I've had a hysterectomy that closed the door to having a baby of my own. But no grief has been as sharp—or as formative—as losing my mother.

I still remember the day my phone rang in April of 2014. It was Good Friday, so the boys were home from school and playing in the backyard, the sound of their little voices laughing and chatting coming through my open bedroom window. Only five short months into marriage, I was soaking in every new part of wife and stepmom life.

I had been matching the largest pile of little socks I ever thought possible that afternoon. I mean, there were so. many. socks. *Always.*

Were they only wearing socks? Were they only changing their socks and re-wearing everything else? I had so many questions as a new stepmom. It was such a vast change from my life as a single woman, yet I loved it.

When my youngest sister's name popped up on my cell phone, I answered, expecting a quick catch-up, maybe even a chance to laugh about all these socks. Instead, her shaky voice delivered four words that would change our worlds forever: *They found a tumor.* As she told me what little she knew, the world ground to a halt.

My mom had gone to her doctor to have him check out some "funny things" that were happening. Thinking she was most likely having gall bladder issues, her family doc scheduled an abdominal ultrasound to confirm. True to form, Mom expected the best possible results. I, likewise, trusted whatever it was would be an easy fix. However, when my sister told me they were going to biopsy the tumor, suspecting pancreatic cancer, I knew immediately the situation was grim. No matter how much I tried not to write a story of how this would go, a deep knowing in my soul set in: *My mom was going to die, probably within the year.*

I could barely catch my breath at the thought of her not being here—wondering how painful this road would be for her, how my dad would be a widower far too young, and how much I needed her now more than ever as I stumbled through the fresh and unfamiliar territory of having a family. She was only sixty-four! A whole lifetime left unwritten.

At one point, with my face in my hands, I heard the little feet of my 6-year-old stepson run down the hallway, pause at my door, and then quickly dart back outside. I tried to collect myself, but the tears wouldn't stop. Only a couple of minutes later, I felt the hesitant touch of an 11-year-old hand on my shoulder, followed by David's sweet little voice whispering, "Kelly … are you ok?"

All I could do was point to my phone and ask him to call his dad. It is so clear to me that God graciously gave me all three of them—Jeremy, David, and JJ—for countless reasons, but especially for this. I don't know how I would have navigated that day, or the season that followed, without them. Those little boys kept me going. There were

Legos to build, games to play, cookies to bake, and laundry (so much laundry!) to do. Their need to keep life moving forward became the very thing that kept *me* moving forward, too.

And then there was Jeremy who held me through it all. His kind, compassionate, loving heart became God's tenderness to me in the darkest, most terrible season of my life. We went from honeymoon stage to the floor of our world dropping out in a single day, but he never once flinched. Somehow, he always managed to be exactly what I needed.

My mom died seven short months later, just five days after our first wedding anniversary. She went through chemo, radiation, a PET scan, biopsies, shunts, and a Whipple procedure. For a moment we thought she might miraculously pull through, but ultimately, she didn't. Before the surgery, while still fighting from home, she stripped everything out of her diet that could possibly cause harm. She choked down smoothies made of broccoli stems and pineapple cores because somewhere, somehow, she heard they might help. She did everything humanly possible to fight this terrible disease. In the end, however, there was nothing more to be done.

Did her efforts extend her life? Perhaps, but I think the real gift of her relentless fight was for those of us she left behind, allowing us to never have to live with the weight of "what ifs."

Following that impossible Good Friday phone call, Jeremy rushed home, and together we drove to the hospital to sit with my mom. Everything shifted that day—we all knew it. You could see it written across every face in the room.

After hugging my mom, Jeremy took the boys to the lobby so I could have a few quiet moments with her. I reached for her hand, looked deep into her eyes, and asked her if she was scared. I will never forget the words that followed ...

"Kelly, I am going to face this with gratitude and thankfulness, and I want you to do the same. Yes, I'm scared, but either way I win. I either get to stay here longer with all of you or I get to go be with Jesus. I'm going to trust God with the road ahead."

Watching my mom walk the road to what ultimately became her death with that kind of confidence in the goodness of God will never be lost on me. For the next seven months, we chose to spend as much time together as we possibly could. Vacations were scheduled. Updated family photos were taken (in superhero t-shirts by the way, with her at the helm as Wonder Woman, of course). And little, semi-insignificant moments became profoundly significant—like when Jeremy, the boys, and I built a treehouse that summer. Because my mom always loved to help, she sat outside with us and tied all the knots for our rope ladder, even though clearly she was exhausted from her treatments. (You better believe we took that ladder with us when we moved the following year when we moved.)

Everything that needed to be said was said. Every hug that could be given was given. We were hoping for the best, but also not taking any chances along the way. The day she went to the hospital for her Whipple procedure—a complex operation for pancreatic cancer—she beamed with joy like she always did as they wheeled her back to the operating room. Her smile always had a way of lighting up the room.

For six more weeks, she fought until, ultimately, her liver tragically failed. I was shattered. How do you go on without a mother—especially after just becoming one yourself? Even though my gut had known this was the likely outcome, grief still took me under like a tidal wave. What followed was a long, dark year. Most days, I felt like I was drowning—yet, by the grace of God, there were moments when I surfaced long enough to catch my breath.

Though I wish with all that I am that she were still here, I've worked hard to carry her spirit forward by choosing joy where I can—because that's what she would want. I make every day count, knowing more fully now how short our time here really is. My heart has stretched wider with empathy and compassion, and I do everything I can to be present with people in their seasons of loss. And because I've walked through grief like this, I feel more equipped to face loss in all its other forms—even in something as small and silly as a garden.

I will not even think to compare powdery mildew with pancreatic cancer—that would be preposterous. I will say, though, that because of losing my mom, I understand more fully that there comes a point that no matter what you do, how hard you fight something, how much you throw at it hoping it can be fixed, many times it's already in motion and can't be undone. In the end, the struggle is less about stopping what's unfolding and more about learning how to face it. A matter of waiting. A matter of surrendering to it all.

Grief never really ends. It softens, shifts, and finds new shapes—but it never disappears. Yet, even in the ache, there are mercies that keep showing up. Little reminders that even when something precious ends, it isn't the whole story.

So, be grateful for the cosmos that linger a few days longer. Thank the dahlias that hold on past their prime. Notice the beauty that breaks through the cracks of loss—because it always does. Look back with gratitude on what bloomed, and look ahead with hope to what's still to come. It won't be the same, and it may not be everything you hoped for—but it will be there. And when it shows up, it will be worth noticing, worth savoring, and without question, worth remembering.

CHAPTER FOURTEEN

STILLNESS IS A SEASON

After everything was torn out of the garden, I remember looking at it and feeling a deep, unexpected sense of pride. That might sound like a funny thing to say, knowing how much I had grieved its loss and beat myself up, feeling responsible for its demise. But the truth is: I had set out to do something new. I chose to be brave despite knowing it could be an utter failure. I listened to myself when I began feeling a pull towards growing cut flowers—and I did the freaking thing. I started scared, uncertain if anything would come from it, and found myself developing resilience in a new way.

Given all the mistakes I made along the journey, it truly felt like a miracle seeing *anything* grow at all. I chose to focus on the beauty that came, not the beauty that didn't—emphasizing the positive, just like my mama taught me.

Before I even ripped everything out, I had already started buying dahlia tubers and seed packets for the next year. Despite the setbacks, slow starts, and sad endings, I was undeniably hooked. And like a good Girl Scout, I was already preparing for my second go, grabbing things from specialty growers and preordering like a maniac. I wanted the good stuff from the people who knew what they were doing—and clearly,

I had already decided I was too fancy for whatever would be available in the spring. Yes, I fully admit I was acting like a dahlia snob before I'd even kept one alive.

Had I told Jeremy? Nope. I wasn't sure he was quite ready to think about another season of growing. After all, he does most of the heavy lifting (I can't carry more than ten pounds—doctor's orders). It's not that I keep him out of major decisions or hide a secret flower credit card—he's just wholeheartedly supportive. I already know his answer will be, "Go for it!" before I even ask. I just like to let my dreams marinate a little before I say them out loud.

Jeremy deserved, and needed, a long winter's nap after all his work during our first growing season—especially before he'd be ready to talk about the next one. Plus, the man loves naps. I'm not lying when I say he's *incredibly* gifted at sleeping. If napping was an Olympic sport, Jeremy would have more medals than Michael Phelps. No question. It's seriously impressive.

So while he napped, I spent time carefully evaluating all I had grown and deciding what I would grow again. Coincidentally, if falling in love with everything you see while seed shopping was also an Olympic sport, I would have my own gold medal, thank you very much.

There were definitely things I didn't want to try again—like calendula, for example. Will someone please help me understand calendula? Are they honestly great cut flowers? I'm not sold on this idea whatsoever. Zinnia and marigolds both seem like such better options. Also, strawflower. Meh. I could take them or leave them. They're basically the fidget spinner of the flower world—fun for a second, but do they really earn their real estate in the garden? Jury's still out for me.

Even after taking calendula and strawflower off the list, I still wanted to add approximately 3,000 more things to the garden in 2024. Which *was* a problem, seeing as we had no plans to expand our growing space. My list was absurdly long and growing by the day as Instagram's algorithm targeted me like a gardening-possessed raccoon let loose in a compost bin full of seed catalogs. I wanted snapdragons, heirloom chrysanthemums, explosion grass, sun ball craspedia, corncockle, bridal crown daffodils, globe thistle, hyacinth, foxtail lilies, and approximately 400 varieties of tulips, give or take.

So … pretty much everything.

Much like the phrase, "Her eyes were bigger than her stomach," my garden dreams were seventeen times larger than our 500 square feet could ever contain. Even barely scratching the surface of cut flower growing taught me that things were about to get wildly, beautifully out of hand.

I made a pact with myself that winter to throw myself into learning the way I had thrown myself into planting. I read books, watched endless YouTube videos, and even signed up for an online course. I devoured everything I could find—only problem being that the more I learned, the more flowers I discovered. It's a slippery slope, I tell you.

I focused on how I could improve: proper soil, drip irrigation vs. overhead watering, the art of succession planting, germination timing, and more. I was a sponge soaking it all in—dreaming of what could be. And not just during the day—quite literally *dreaming* of it.

In the stillness of winter, even my dreams bloomed. I would be transported to expansive fields, surrounded by flowers of every kind— the sky above me blue, the wind blowing softly through the blooms, butterflies fluttering and landing to feast. And sometimes—when I was extra lucky—my beloved black Labrador retriever Zoey would be at my feet, panting softly.

Zoey had always loved walking through the landscaping beds in our front yard, plopping all 85 pounds of herself right smack in the middle of everything. She'd keep me company while I weeded or snipped arrangements for Ezra, flattening anything in her way. It always made me smile, even when there were literal flower casualties in her wake.

Toward the end, she insisted on returning to the house only by way of the flower beds—altogether boycotting the sidewalk. She would linger slowly, weaving through celosia and coral bells, salvia and lilies. We'd try to hurry her along, but she just ignored us and took it all in at her deliberate pace—enjoying them just as much as I did. In her own way, Zoey was teaching me the gift of slowing down.

I know she would have loved the cut flower garden expansion, but she sadly left us right before everything started growing. Her thirteen-year-old body had lived just as long as it could.

So sometimes, when I sleep, my heart puts her in the garden with me. And I smile—grateful, even in dreams, for the faintest idea she's been with me.

One of the most beautiful and unexpected things that happened last summer was when our other dog, Mumford—a rescue pup we got for the boys' birthdays years ago—suddenly wanted to be in the garden with me. Up until then, he'd shown zero interest. He was more of a blanket-burrito type, perfectly content keeping JJ company at the foot of his bed during Netflix marathons. But something shifted. As Jeremy and I made our evening rounds through the garden, Mumford began following us. Then he started settling in, carving out a little home for himself among the flowers. Whenever I went outside, he wanted to be there, too. It was the sweetest thing.

He'd walk in, find an open patch, and carefully curl up—never once crushing a bloom, a courtesy Zoey would *never* have offered. This still makes me laugh because, personality-wise, you'd expect the opposite. Yet there he was, steady and gentle, becoming my constant garden companion in the wake of losing Zo-Zo. It felt a little like he'd been quietly watching her all along, waiting for his turn to step in and carry the mantle she left behind.

You know how dogs lose their minds when you grab *the shoes*—the ones that mean it's time for a W-A-L-K? Mumford started reacting that way to *my overalls*. I wore them nearly every day like the stylish suburban micro-flower farmer that I am. The second I stepped into them, he'd unroll from his blanket burrito and head straight for the door. It was ridiculous and endearing, all at once.

Those overalls quickly became my official gardening uniform, just as I expected. Erin Benzakein knows what's up. And if that woman can pull them off, I'm sure going to try to as well—even if I end up looking like the garden version of Celeste Barber in the process. Either way, I'll gladly pull them back out next season, buttoning them up each morning with my snips in hand and a bucket of fresh water in the other, ready to harvest whatever blooms await me.

With the first growing season in the rearview mirror, we closed the garden gate and called it a wrap. After a long winter's nap, we'd be back at it with a little more experience and a little more wisdom.

Well … at least, that's what we thought. The garden, as always, had other plans.

CHAPTER FIFTEEN

GO FORTH AND BE AWESOME

Every day growing up, as my sisters and I would walk out to the bus and leave for school, my dad would ever-so-casually declare "Another day in which to excel!"—then wave cheerfully, sending us on our way. That's literally word-for-word what he said instead of "Bye! Hope you have a great day at school!" like most normal dads. I both loved him for it (secretly, of course) and shook my head in opposition as I would leave, knowing he actually meant it.

My parents raised us to be people who not only sought excellence but achieved it. We Jackson Sisters unequivocally knew our report cards were to be full of A's, not because our folks were unreasonable or outlandishly demanding, but rather because they knew we were capable of getting them. Anything less would reflect a lack of trying, an inexcusable violation in the Jackson household. School was our job, and in our house, we did jobs with our complete selves. There was no half-assing anything. Ever. Nay, we put our whole asses into whatever the task was at hand.

I find it equal parts hilarious and annoying how much we involuntarily become our parents as we age. Try as you might to be an individual, some reflexes just show up out of nowhere, and—*cue the dramatic reveal*—one day you've become *them*. Shortly into stepmomming, I would drop our youngest off at elementary school. Wouldn't you know, as JJ opened the car door and I waved goodbye, I intentionally had to bite my tongue, or "Another day in which to excel!" would have come spewing out? I felt it welling up as I approached the drop-off zone every single time.

After a few close calls, I decided I needed to adjust the phrase a bit and make it feel more "laid-back stepmom" and less "former-Marine dad." So one day, as I drove up and stopped for him to get out, I decided to try out the revised version I'd formulated. "Go forth and be awesome!" I said. And JJ, without missing a beat, responded, "That's a lot of pressure, Kelly. How about I just try to be average?" Touché, kid. And so "Go forth and be average!" officially became my parting well-wish at school drop off.

Though there is absolutely nothing wrong with being average, my parents raised all three of their daughters to always go for gold. They instilled in us so much belief that we could do anything—and for that, I am so profoundly grateful. I still find myself often hearing the echoes of their well-wishes from decades ago, cheering me on, assuring me I can do whatever I'm attempting, and encouraging me to give it my all in the process.

I hope people will know and remember me as one who lived life fully and abundantly, always dreaming big dreams and loving others with my whole heart. One who belly laughed often and cried when it mattered—letting the mess and magic be all mixed together. And, I want my life to encourage others to do the same—to be a kind of living permission slip that they should just go for it, shoot for the moon, and believe in themselves along the way. Not just the safe thing. Not just the practical thing. Not just the "what would make sense on paper" thing. But the wildly beautiful, makes you nervous, has a 50% chance of flopping but a 100% chance of making you feel alive thing. Because honestly, too many people are walking around with "Go forth and be average!" energy—not in the funny, childlike way JJ meant it, but in the grown-up, self-protective way. I get it. Failure is rarely fun. However, it breaks my heart that somewhere along the way, failure became this big, scary monster instead of what it actually is: proof that you *showed up*. That you cared enough to try, didn't shrink when you could have, and had the guts to put something out into the world when it would've been so much easier to play it safe.

Somewhere along the way, we've started measuring our lives by how polished they appear instead of how fully they're lived. I'll quickly blame modern-day culture for throwing gasoline on the fire. We've got Pinterest boards full of kitchens where not a single dirty dish exists, reels of curated mornings that somehow feature zero under-eye bags, and Instagram filters that can make even a pile of laundry look aspirational. We've built this false standard of "success" that's aesthetic first, honesty second. And while I love a good visual (hello, former photographer here), I worry how often people are quietly deciding that their life, their dream, or their effort just falls short. So they step back and play small, or they shelve the dream entirely. Not because they don't want it, but because they're terrified of being seen trying and not reaching the moon.

But what if simply trying is the most important part? What if the beauty's in the reaching—even if your hands come back empty? What would happen if we stopped tying our worth to outcomes and started anchoring it in the bravery it takes even to begin?

Because failure isn't the opposite of success, it's how you earn wisdom. It's the scar that proves you were in the ring. And sometimes it's the divine detour that leads you to a place even better than the one you mapped out.

Don't be afraid to be seen trying. Don't choose small just because it feels safer. Dream big. Love bigger. Fall on your face if you have to—but at least fall forward. And when you do, get back up, brush off your knees, and maybe even laugh at yourself. You have to. Honestly, I laugh at myself more than anyone.

After my first year of growing cut flowers, I simply cannot imagine my life now without them. Specifically, not growing them. It will forever be a part of me. But would you believe me if I told you I entered my second year a bit … afraid? I started my first year knowing it could all fail. I ended that year having learned how nature wants to find a way to thrive, even despite me.

But what if year two was different? What if, even after everything I had learned, I somehow ended up less successful? What would that say about me? What would people think? All of these thoughts came flooding into my brain as I pulled out the seeds and trays and got to work implementing my plans. I felt like my critics (the rent-free tenants in my brain, not actual people) had more riding on the outcome of year two. Meanwhile, however, my inner cheerleaders were enthusiastically waving their pom-poms, convinced I could pull off something even better.

I had two choices: Cave to the critics or bet on myself. We all face those choices—probably more often than we realize. But when you really stop and think about it, caving to fear never leads to joy. No one looks back with gratitude for the chances they *didn't* take. Playing it safe only closes doors and sets the stage for regret. And honestly? Playing it safe is the riskiest move of all.

Courage is simply a redefined relationship with fear. I know firsthand that courage doesn't eliminate fear—it just shows fear its place. To experience the joy and beauty of my garden again required me to put fear in the backseat. I had to maintain control of the wheel from start to finish, or the beauty I hoped to cultivate would never gain traction and find its way into the world.

So I started. Again. And I did it afraid. Fear was still yapping away, but I decided not to listen. Instead, I followed my heart as it tugged me toward another season of growth, filling my mind with images of what could be and all the beauty waiting for me in the messy, enthusiastic yes to year two.

Shocking as it might be, I once again ordered at least three times as many seeds as I could fit in our garden, so determining which I would ultimately use was a painful process. Once I had a decent idea of what I would attempt to grow and approximately how many of each, I mapped it all out using the trusty graph paper template Jeremy made me the year before. Then, an oversized wall calendar was purchased, and Saturdays for the next several months were quickly notated with what seeds needed to be started, when seedlings would need to be hardened off, and when I would transplant things into the garden.

I had learned the year before not to sow them all on the same day, let alone too late in the game, so the calendar directed when the grand juggling act should begin—as well as how it should unfold.

At the beginning of January, the grow lights were turned on again, still secured in their spots on the metal shelves in the basement from the year prior. The new heat mats I learned we needed were acquired. They were then laid out in position, awaiting the series of trays to come as the orchestration of it all began. Things were looking *very legit*, if I do say so myself.

I felt so much more prepared. After watching multiple YouTube videos over the winter, I did not simply buy the premade seed starting soil I'd used the year before, but instead set out to make Blossom and Branch's "peat-free soil recipe" made from products even my favorite local nursery didn't stock. I found the coco coir there (basically shredded coconut husks that help hold moisture), but we also needed green sand (a mineral amendment to boost nutrients) and Coco Loco (a fancy soil mix that's part compost, part magic pixie dust). Those things, apparently, were only sold at hydroponic supply stores. Jeremy and I called ahead to our selected location and confirmed everything was in stock. When we walked in later, I'm 10,000% confident we were the only ones in the establishment not looking to grow cannabis. After all my research, however, I knew the way seeds started mattered. So if buying seed soil supplies in a store for weed growers was what was required, I was going to do it, dang it.

After the soil was mixed and the initial seeds were sown, the grow light timer was set, and the trays got their eight needed hours of rest each night. The heat mats were turned on and the humidity domes were put in place until little sprouts started appearing. I waited until 70% of them were showing signs of life, and then the mats were turned off and the humidity domes were put away. I bought Neptune's Harvest organic fish fertilizer, recommended by many online, to feed the seedlings as they grew, and made sure to do so every other week like clockwork. We even set up a fan nearby to mimic the wind.

The difference between year one and year two was night and day. Seedlings were thriving and, at times, outgrowing their trays. They were no longer itty-bitty, teeny-weeny seedlings. They were seedlings who embraced each day as another in which to excel. At one point, I even had to pinch off the snapdragons I was trying for the first time as they grew so tall they touched the grow lights. Not only did I have to pinch them back—I learned that I could dip the pinched-off portions in rooting hormone and start a whole new tray, nearly doubling my expected output. Y'all, I felt like a girl who actually knew what she was doing.

Meanwhile, the 250 tulip and daffodil bulbs we'd planted the previous November began poking through the soil—mainly serving as a reminder that I did *not* have it all figured out, as the first problems of season two started to appear. Suddenly, the whole thing felt shaky again. Some shoots came up stunted. Some never came up at all. Others looked suspiciously like the squirrels had made dinner plans. It was a gentle nudge whispering, *"Hey, remember? You're still learning."*

With growth, there is no finish line—you never fully arrive. Not really. Even when you know more. Even when you *are* more. Something new, something unpredictable, something humbling awaits you right around every corner. Fear will still show up. Mistakes will still get made. But that doesn't mean you're failing. It just means you're growing. The question isn't, "Will I be scared again?" It's, "Will I keep going anyway?" Because the only way to keep uncovering joy is to keep moving toward it—one tiny, trembling, hopeful step at a time.

Sometimes you grow the most in the second season—not because it's easier, but because it's *harder*. Because you show up without the novelty or the wide-eyed wonder—and you do it anyway. That's grit. Maybe that's what year two is really about—not recreating what worked, but trusting that who you are becoming matters more than what you produce. That faithfulness guides better than perfection. That courage doesn't reside in confidence—it's forged in commitment.

Start anyway.
Even if you're scared.
Especially if you're scared.

You might not know everything, but you know enough to begin. Coincidentally? That's always when beauty takes root.

CHAPTER SIXTEEN

ALL OR NOTHING, ALWAYS

Even though I *believed* I had exercised remarkable restraint while ordering spring bulbs, we somehow ended up with over a dozen varieties—and not just a dozen bulbs, but a dozen *types*. If you've ever fallen down the rabbit hole of specialty bulb shopping, you know. You go in thinking you'll grab a tasteful mix of daffodils and tulips and come out the other side sweating over whether you need two or three kinds of fringed parrot tulips (you need three). Honestly, I could have ordered thousands and still felt like I was leaving too many behind.

So while I was feeling pretty smug about "only" having 250 bulbs to plant, Jeremy just stood there, blinking slowly—equal parts awe and mild terror—wondering how this had become his life. Every time a padded envelope would arrive in the mail, he would examine it like a TSA agent spotting something suspicious—also somehow knowing full well this wasn't the last of it.

Look—I am well aware that I can be … a bit much. That square's been marked off on my personal bingo card for years. My personality is set to "max" at all times. It's a virtue when I need it to be, a vice when I forget to eat lunch. I'm not planting one herb pot, I'm orchestrating a full-scale reenactment of *Versailles, but make it Zone 6b hardy*. (USDA Plant Hardiness Zones are like climate cheat sheets. Zone 6b hardy = gardener code for "this plant can handle a Midwest winter tantrum without needing a heated blanket and a prayer circle.")

And yes, it exhausts people. Sometimes it even exhausts me. But I also grew up with a dad who believed that every day was "another day in which to excel," and I apparently absorbed that like gospel. So if I show up to life like it's the Olympic trials for hobby gardening—well, I blame nurture, not nature.

When I say I'm extreme, I mean I'm reliably, predictably, consistently extreme. If I dip a toe in, it's probably just to check the temperature before I cannonball. And if I'm going to cannonball, I'm bringing 250 bulbs with me.

My mom used to love telling the story of how, during college, I once came home for a long weekend and decided I wanted to bake homemade banana bread for all of my new friends. And not just a slice for each of them. No—in my classic all-or-nothing fashion, I decided the only acceptable way forward was to bake *an entire loaf for each person*. Obviously.

Banana bread, my absolute favorite of the baked goods my mom would send in care packages, tucked alongside quarters for laundry and a handwritten note, made me know she was thinking of me and loved me enough to send me a taste of home. So naturally, I wanted to share that feeling with every single one of my new friends.

Being a textbook Enneagram 2 (translation: I basically always come armed with cookies and unsolicited encouragement), I've been described—lovingly—as "aggressively generous." So when I came home for that notorious three-day weekend in college, it was very on brand of me to declare upon arrival my intention to make excessive amounts of banana bread during my short, three-day weekend home. My parents rolled their eyes, but they knew resistance was futile. So for 72 hours, my mom's kitchen became the world's least efficient commercial bakery. When I left, the backseat of my car held two dozen freshly baked loaves, and the unmistakable scent of someone who means well just a little *too* hard.

In my thirties, I swapped banana bread for themed birthday parties. Because—and I stand by this—your birthday is the one day of the year you can invite people to do something mildly unhinged, and no one can say no. You get a free pass, and I used mine with gusto. I mean … who's gonna say no to the birthday girl?

Each party had a theme, and every detail matched—attire, food, drinks, décor, music. Thankfully, most of my friends didn't just roll with it; they went all in. When I turned 31, I purchased a pint of every Baskin-Robbins ice cream flavor, and my friends sampled them all night like it was their job. When I was in my two-stepping era, everyone met up at a local country bar called Denim & Diamonds and showed up boot-scootin' ready. The year I threw a supermodel party, a friend of mine came as a Calvin Klein underwear model and literally walked around all night in nothing but boxer briefs. (Epic.) Every detail, every year was lit up in neon or doused in glitter.

I still consistently look for ways to make everything from dinner parties to holiday events as over-the-top as possible. Take when our oldest left for the Navy and we threw him a pirate party. (Yes … we know Navy sailors aren't pirates.) Were there giant letters stuck into our yard spelling out "Ahoy Matey" the day of said party? Yes, of course there were. Was the soundtrack to *Pirates of the Caribbean* playing on loop all night? You betcha. Did I happen to hire a grown man who came dressed as an actual pirate—with a *live* parrot on his shoulder? Heck yeah, I did. I mean … have you even thrown a pirate party until a hyacinth macaw has flown around your living room? I vote no. That bird acted like it owned the place. And honestly, it kind of did.

So when that first bulb planting day rolled around, of course there were over 250 bulbs eager to get nestled underground for a long winter's nap. Jeremy, not being surprised at this point after 10 years of marriage, had prepared by buying what I affectionately called a "mini auger" to attach to his drill (no precursor call required). This little attachment made bulb planting such a breeze that we knocked out getting them in the ground faster than I had planned. Jeremy was delighted. I found myself wishing I had ordered more.

I *especially* wished I had ordered more when spring arrived and my sweet tulips became the first target of attack for the bunnies. They were back, and you'd have thought I was growing Dove chocolate by how fast they annihilated the plants. Once again, I found myself at the local nursery shopping in the "please stop the bunnies" section. Did you know they make sprays that smell like pepper? Sprays that smell like predator urine? Sprays made of actual predator urine? There are pellets, shiny things, slow-release formulas … the bunny battle is clearly a shared trauma amongst gardeners everywhere.

I picked a few options and tried to make my few remaining tulip hopefuls less appealing to the furry jerks. And wouldn't you know it? Some survived. Well, at least technically they did, but they only grew a few inches out of the ground—no stems to speak of whatsoever. Just a puff of chewed-off leaves and a sad little bud practically sitting on the dirt like it had given up halfway through the assignment.

Apparently, I needed something called "shade cover" for them. Or maybe they weren't getting enough water? I had become a member of a few flower-growing groups on Facebook over the last year. After posting a couple of photos, I received a dozen different suggestions to help me be, and I quote, "more successful next year." All I could think was, "Like there will be a next year," followed by "Why is it so freaking hard to grow everything?" and then, "If this is the start of year two, Lord help me." Gardening has a way of keeping you humble, that's for sure.

I will say one of the best parts of being so extreme is the occasional big win after you've gone all in. After carefully planting that small lot of tulip bulbs, I had pictured my yard erupting into something out of Amsterdam—a rainbow of fruit flavor rising up in defiance of winter. Bold color. Full stems. Drama. Glory.

Instead, I felt like Zoolander watching Will Ferrell's Mugatu present me with "The Derek Zoolander Center for Tulips Who Can't Grow Good." What were they? Tulips for ants? They needed to be at least … three times bigger than this.

Buying and subsequently planting 250 bulbs was for sure a "chips all in" move on my end. But instead of winning big, I lost hard. And though this sounds dramatic, I was crushed. Not just because it was a financial investment (though it was also that), but because

I buried so much hope with those bulbs. And hope, as it turns out, doesn't come with a money-back guarantee, either.

In true form, I responded to the disappointment with appropriate subtlety: by vowing I would *never* grow tulips again. This was a full swoon-on-a-fainting-couch situation—hand to forehead, breathless and tragic, as if I had just been personally betrayed by the entire genus *Tulipa*. "Henceforth," I declared dramatically to no one in particular, "Tulips are dead to me." (End scene.)

We'll see if time changes my mind. It usually does. Time has this special way of sanding down the sharp edges of frustration until things don't feel quite so personal anymore. The sting dulls. You start to romanticize ideals again. But for now, tulips have been demoted to the floral version of an ex I'm not ready to be friends with. Gorgeous? Yes. But I'm still giving them the cold shoulder until further notice.

And as for the bunnies? Even though I'm tempted to wish them dead (that would simplify gardening tremendously), I don't want to come across sounding like a cartoon villain with a vendetta against woodland creatures. So, let's just say we're still working on boundaries.

CHAPTER SEVENTEEN

YOU'RE NOT ALWAYS GOING TO SUCK THIS BAD

Thankfully, as my first attempt at a cut tulip harvest proved to be a total bust, massive wins were happening down in the basement. The seedlings were thriving. We were nearing our final frost date, and some plants were so eager they had already started budding in their trays. I was trying my hand at pre-sprouting ranunculus and sweet peas for the first time (translation: tucking them into damp soil early, essentially tricking them into thinking it's go-time before it actually is). Jeremy was researching irrigation systems. Tubers were starting to arrive in the mail, as always eliciting more side eye from my husband (bless). We were finding our rhythm again—still wobbling a bit, but at least learning the steps.

While I was still slightly devastated by the tulip situation (RIP, bite-sized floral tapas for rabbits), I also knew we didn't have time to sit and pout. Not in spring. There's too much to do. Everything is in motion—a living, breathing symphony that's already warming up. Miss a cue, and you risk missing the best stanza of the whole dang song.

Back in fourth grade, my parents for some reason insisted I join the elementary school orchestra. They told me to pick an instrument, so I chose the cello. They told me to pick something smaller. I said I wanted to play the cello. They said again, "Smaller." I repeated, "Cello." My mom, who knew full well she'd be the one hauling this thing to rehearsals, changed tactics and told me to choose between the violin and viola. And what fourth grader *chooses* the viola? Answer: My sister Dana, though I'm reasonably sure her choice was the result of painfully having to listen to me learn the violin. Notably, my other sister, Janel, *also* decided not to play the violin.

Have you ever heard a 10-year-old learn to play violin? It's basically the auditory version of a migraine. Squeaks, screeches, accidental wonky harmonics. It even hurt *me*. The more I played, the more I regretted not fighting harder for the cello. Sure, it would have had its own learning curve—but at least it was pitched low enough that our dog would have most likely not run away from it.

Later that year, after months of squeaking and squawking as I pushed through the initial stages of learning, we participated in something our school district called the *Festival of Strings*. All the orchestras— fourth grade through high school—played in succession on the high school gym floor. The fourth graders kicked it off. Then the fifth graders. Then sixth. Then junior high. Then, finally, the high school symphony orchestra.

You could hear the progression with every group—how the squeaking gave way to skill, how the awkwardness smoothed into intention. It was honestly pretty inspiring—especially to anyone who knew (or was) a fourth-grade violinist. It was truly the kindest, most creative way of communicating without words, "You're not always going to suck this bad. Keep going."

I didn't quit the orchestra, but I sure did quit the violin. Ironically, after all that talk from my parents about choosing a *smaller* instrument, I switched from playing the violin ... to playing the string bass. This was not, I promise, an act of defiance. I didn't set out to one-up the situation with my parents, I swear. Instead, my switching to string bass was motivated that night at Festival of Strings by a high school senior who played bass as if it was her birthright. She was the only girl in a long row of bass players, and they gave her a coveted annual award, naming her the most inspiring student in the orchestra that year.

I watched her play with passion and skill, completely spellbound, and found myself more interested in playing the bass in twenty minutes than I ever had been in playing the violin.

So I became a bass player. I loved that instrument so much I even earned a small music scholarship to play in my university's orchestra—which never, ever would have happened if I'd stuck with the violin ... or probably even the cello.

Do I still play now? Not at all. I haven't touched a bass in decades. But those years changed how I hear things. I came to understand the genius of a perfectly timed crescendo. I hear the subtle beauty in the transition from the wind section quieting right as the string section takes the lead. I notice the fullness of sound that comes from an ensemble of musicians playing everything from the string bass to the piccolo, and I truly find delight in it. My ears have been trained to appreciate the nuances of it all, and my heart naturally follows suit.

As a result, every year when winter finally fades and spring starts stretching its legs, I find myself watching the progression of nature—first sunny yellow daffodils, then deep purple iris, then pink pillowy peonies—and ultimately hear a melody unfolding. It's like a carefully orchestrated handoff, each bloom stepping aside just as the next takes the stage. The garden becomes a living score, layers building as the season goes on.

And I'm struck by the fact that somehow, I get to be part of it. Not as the soloist or the conductor—and definitely not first-chair. But I'm in the mix, playing my little background part. Adding a tiny bit of harmony to something so much bigger than me, and that's kind of the magic of it all.

This is why I say there wasn't time to sulk about the tulips. Their little piccolo solo was fleeting and honestly a little off-key ... but maybe that was the point. Sometimes the thing you buried your hopes with doesn't pan out—the job, the friendship, the big moment. Yet you want to stick with it, try to fix it, or feel bad about it a little longer. Life, however, is always queuing up what's next. The invitation isn't to stay in the stanza that disappointed you. The invitation is to keep showing up for the rest of the music.

I used to think success was nailing every note. These days? I think it's just staying in the song—even when your part sounds like a cat fight in a back alley. It's pulling weeds after the tulips flop. Planting anyway. Getting back in the dirt even after something sucker-punched your heart.

It's the slow, stubborn courage to keep going—even when you botch your solo so badly that the entire room collectively winces in unison. But frankly, that's what growth usually sounds like—not some sweeping movie soundtrack with the music swelling at the perfect moment, but a squeaky middle school recital where half the kids forgot their sheet music, the other half are playing a full measure behind, and somebody's mom is crying with joy in the bleachers. It's awkward, off-beat, occasionally painful, weirdly endearing—but it's still progress.

Just like a fourth-grader learning to play violin, we're all invited to be beginners at something. You don't get to skip that stage just because you're an adult with a mortgage and lower back pain. Whether it's growing flowers or starting anew after any failure, it's going to be clunky before it's beautiful. Full stop.

You'll plant things that never bloom. You'll chase dreams that ghost you without so much as a "thanks for trying." You'll pour your heart into something that completely bombs and leaves you wondering if you're actually cut out for this. But that doesn't mean it wasn't worth doing, and it certainly doesn't mean you're not getting better.

If you're in a season where everything feels off-key and you're one emotional hiccup away from chucking your metaphorical violin out the nearest window (and legitimately, who would blame you?), please hear me loud and clear: You're not always going to suck this bad. Promise. Just keep playing.

CHAPTER EIGHTEEN

THAT WAS THEN, THIS IS NOW

The ranunculus were the first ones ready to find their way outside. It had been a weird spring in Kansas City—temperatures all over the place—so I decided to plant them in pots, figuring I could drag them back inside if Mother Nature pulled one of her "just kidding, it's winter again" stunts. I had high hopes for those ranunculus, perhaps unreasonably so. Orange ranunculus was a star player in our wedding flowers—no small feat considering we got married in November. There's something so magical about their layers-on-layers of petals, the way they open slowly for days like they're revealing secrets. And their vase life? Stop it. They really are the gift that keeps on giving.

I babied those pre-sprouted ranunculus corms for weeks (corms are weird little nuggets that look like shriveled up tiny octopus but are hiding *serious* glow-up potential). Yet the night before I expected to cut my very first blooms, deer broke into my fenced garden and helped themselves to a little floral snicky snack.

You might be thinking, "Don't you live in the suburbs?" Yes, we do, but we also live just a little too close to a creek, which means the local deer consider our backyard part of their HOA. We've caught them lounging back there like they pay rent and met them in the driveway with that telltale "Oh, hey, you live here too?" headlight stare. We've even seen them grazing on our cul-de-sac island like it's a Whole Foods sample station. The audacity.

That morning, I walked out ready to harvest five promising buds—my first ranunculus, ever—only to find them chewed down to the stem. Just stumps, surrounded by hoofprints.

Let's be clear: I only had five buds to begin with. I was a first-year ranunculus grower and as per usual, didn't really know what I was doing. Eight weeks earlier, I had soaked the twenty corms I purchased in still tap water, which may not seem like that big of a deal, but apparently, as I later found out, you shouldn't. Upon further investigation, the water, according to those who know more about it than I do, needs to remain fresh and oxygenated. (I couldn't make this stuff up if I tried.) I don't think I had oversoaked them, but evidentially that's a possibility, too. Supposedly, over soaking can promote fungal growth, so that's great. And if it's too warm, the corms can rot. If it's Tuesday and Mercury is in retrograde, they might just pack up and die out of spite. I swear it's astounding anything ever grows at all after reading all of this very detailed information online.

So yes, the fact that I had five thriving plants felt like a small miracle. And yes, it was devastating to walk out and find my miracle had been eaten by the neighborhood snack patrol. I imagined that deer waiting. Watching. Holding out for just the right moment—like people hovering for the next batch of fresh rotisserie chickens at Costco. Or dieters on February 1st after finishing the Whole30 in January.

I was batting zero so far in year two. How could it be worse than the first? In my growing station in the basement, everything appeared to be going so much better than the summer before, and yet so much of what was happening outside was not. To make things worse, it all felt completely out of my control.

There comes a point when you can only do what you can do. I mean, I've seen deer fencing, but that twelve-foot-tall eyesore is not happening in my suburban lawn. No one would be okay with that—not even me. Sadly, our humble three-and-a-half-foot fence was basically a neon sign declaring, *"All-you-can-eat garden bar. No cover charge."*

I was frustrated, but then I remembered another of my mom's go-to phrases. She had a few—always loving, always honest, and always delivered with a kind of gentle authority that made it impossible to argue. My mom was a woman of compassion and grace, but she also had a way of saying it like it was when you needed to hear it. If it wasn't her signature, *"Emphasize the positive,"* it was probably, *"That was then. This is now. We're moving on."* I know. They're both so annoying. I hated it almost every time she would say either. And yet, undoubtedly every time she did, the woman was right.

You sure can focus on how things *were* for a whole long time, can't you? But does it change the result of them being what they are now? Rarely, if ever. My deer-eaten ranunculus is a prime example. I could stand in my garden obsessing over what should have bloomed, should have worked, should have survived. But none of that changed the fact that it didn't. At some point, you have to stop holding funerals for what *didn't* bloom and just get back to planting.

That was then. This is now.

I was faced with a decision. There I stood at bat in season two with two big strikes so far. I could throw the towel in and say, "I'm done. This is dumb. I'll never beat the deer and rabbits." I could half-ass my swing at the next ball, get a grounder, and never make it to first base. Or, I could walk up to that plate and ready myself to swing for a homer.

The tulips had flopped. The ranunculus were toast. But there were a dozen dahlia tubers waiting in the wings, irrigation lines going in, and a basement full of seedlings ready to shine. One could argue I was actually swinging for a grand slam.

I didn't swing because I was sure I'd win.
I swung because there was still a chance to play.

That's what we forget sometimes: The goal isn't always the win. Sometimes, it's just staying in the game. Taking one more swing. Giving one more yes.

Imagine what would have happened if I had given up on love right before meeting Jeremy. Thank God I chose to go on one more first date. Imagine if I had given up on finding fulfilling work after my photography career had ended. Sure, I was disappointed, but I looked for another way to be creative and found something beautiful.

That's what I had to do in the garden, too. Even after rabbits. Even after deer. Even after not knowing what I was doing (again). I felt the disappointment, took time to acknowledge the hurt, but ultimately shrugged it off and stepped up to the plate again.

That was then. This is now.
And now always holds possibility.

You might be staring at the shredded remains of something you were really hopeful about. Maybe it's a dream job that ghosted you after three rounds of interviews. Maybe it's a relationship that fizzled without explanation. Maybe it's the house you didn't get, the side hustle that never took off, the new city that didn't feel like home, the thing you *really* thought was going to bloom this time—and didn't.

Feel the sting. Let yourself sulk for a minute. Curse the sky and announce that you are officially retired from hope. Effective immediately. Benefits pending.

But only for a minute.

You can replay the what-ifs and should-have-beens all day, but it won't rewrite the story. What you *can* do is take one more swing. Even if you're limping. Even if your heart's a little bruised. Even if your confidence is hanging on by a thread.

You're not out of the game. Not even close. You get the chance to try again. And again and again and again if need be.

That was then.
This is now.
We're moving on.

CHAPTER NINETEEN

FLOWER DOULA

Ironically, just as my tulips were flopping and my ranunculus were being turned into doe hors d'oeuvres, friends started reaching out to say, "Hey … I think I want to grow flowers, too." They'd followed along on Instagram during my first season—watching the chaos unfold in real time: the bug infestations, the surprise successes, the drama, the dirt, the deer. Apparently, instead of thinking, *This woman has lost it,*" they thought, *"That actually looks kind of fun."* Bold choice.

These friends were clear they didn't want to do it on the scale I had (smart). One had an unused corner in her backyard. Another wanted to sneak a few blooms into her vegetable garden. Neither had big ambitions—no pop-up bouquet sales or farmers markets—they just wanted to try something new. They both said versions of the same thing: "I have no idea what I'm doing." To which I said: "Same. Let's do it anyway." I knew, however, if I ended up with armloads of flowers after all I had done wrong, they could jump in and find success as well. It might not all grow, but something would.

I jokingly started calling myself their flower doula, which really just meant I sent dramatic texts like "YOU'VE GOT THIS!" and talked them off the ledge when Japanese beetles showed up for the first time like the tiny green punks they are. I answered questions about soil and seeds and sunlight, celebrated their first sprouts like a proud aunt, and sent entirely too many links to things I wish I had known earlier.

Here's what surprised me: I actually had answers—and many of them were kind of good. It honestly gave me confidence as I stood at the plate with two strikes on the board. After the two blows I already faced, to be reminded how much more I knew going into summer number two could not have been more perfectly timed. Every time I reminded *them* they could do it, I heard myself saying it and took the words to heart myself.

Somewhere between Googling *"why are my Bells of Ireland yellowing"* and scolding baby bunnies, I'd picked up a decent sense of what works and what doesn't. I still didn't know everything (not even close), but I knew enough. When someone texts you a photo of a drooping seedling and you can confidently reply, *"cut back on watering,"* and you're actually right? That's basically the nerdiest imaginary badge of honor I've ever earned. (But could I actually get a badge? I would sew that puppy on my overalls immediately, please and thank you.)

Helping them helped me remember: I'm not where I was. I've learned, and I've grown. I may not be the calm, compost-rich matriarch I someday aspire to be, but I've got lived experience—and sometimes lived experience is the most generous thing you can offer.

I think we underestimate how much we have to offer people. We dismiss ourselves because we're not "experts" or we don't think we have enough wisdom or know how to help someone else. But think of it from their perspective. Seeing someone take a step in a direction they're interested in going is sometimes all it takes for them to muster up the confidence to try it themselves. Or maybe they weren't even interested in the first place, but in watching someone else experience joy and beauty through traveling or baking sourdough or learning to play pickleball or starting a garden, they suddenly find themselves curious whether they might find joy and beauty in doing those things, too.

Our hearts long for joy. Our souls crave beauty. Being someone who offers even the slightest amount of assurance that it can be done feeds some of the deepest needs in others who watch cautiously from the sidelines. Fear oftentimes talks people out of first steps. It convinces them that "not-doing" is safer. But what most people actually need isn't an expert—they just need someone who remembers what it feels like to start. They need someone who can say, "Yeah, that part's confusing. Here's what worked for me." They need someone to normalize the panic. To be proof that it's not only *possible*, but it's allowed to be *messy* along the way. They need someone to say, "Yes, you will absolutely mess things up. Do it anyway."

We all need our own personal version of a flower doula.
And sometimes, shockingly, we are one—without even realizing it.

There is something deeply beautiful about cheering someone else on while you're still in the thick of it. Still figuring it out and even limping a little from your last mistake. It's not about having it all together—it's about being willing to walk alongside someone else while *you're* still walking it out, too.

The ripple effect of courage can be massive. Watching someone chase their unique curiosities can spark bravery in us, which in turn becomes the encouragement another person needs to step out, too. Also, the more we practice courage, the more willing we are to risk again. It's like a muscle—strengthened over time until it begins to outpower the brain that's wired to keep us safe. Our minds talk us out of risk, but our souls call us into the unknown—awakening us to beauty we'd never find without courage.

Seeing someone else try—even awkwardly, even imperfectly—unlocks something in us. It makes the dream feel more possible. It makes the fear feel somewhat shared. And when you watch another person do the thing you thought was too big or too scary, suddenly it doesn't feel so far out of reach anymore.

I find people like Erin of Floret Flower Farm inspiring, not just because of where she is today—owning acres of land in the Pacific Northwest with a staff harvesting her unique, hybridized seeds—but because she shares with us, step by step, how she got there. At one point, she was a mom of two little ones growing what she could in a tiny backyard.

Little by little, with passion and perseverance, she built her business into what it is now. She didn't always have the massive production she runs today. It started with a young mom who bravely took her first step—with curiosity, courage, and just enough tenacity to keep going.

That's what drew me into this crazy adventure, and what helps me stay the course. Not because she was perfect when she started—but because she *wasn't*.

Let me be clear: We aren't all called to be Erin Benzakeins or Martha Stewarts or Ina Gartens. I, however, want to be the best version of me—brave, scrappy, generous, wildly imperfect, and willing to show up anyway. I want to choose courage over fear at every turn, never letting anything keep me from the joy and beauty my heart was made to experience. And if my choosing courage somehow frees others to pursue what their own hearts are calling them to, that's when the joy really multiplies.

So when my friends reach out and ask, "Am I too late to plant zinnias?" I get to be the one to say, "You're right on time. You've totally got this."

Watching someone say yes to *their* thing—even if it's completely different than yours—can be the spark that lights up something in you. Whether it's flowers or painting or learning to roller skate in your forties, witnessing someone else's joy is sometimes enough to help you reach for your own.

So be the person who says yes.
Because courage is a muscle.
The more you use it—even clumsily—the stronger it gets.

Before you know it, someone will look at your chaotic, joy-filled, bug-bitten garden and say, "I think I want to try, too." And you'll text back, without missing a beat: "YOU'VE GOT THIS!" Because apparently, you're someone's flower doula now, too.

CHAPTER TWENTY

WHERE THE WILD THINGS GREW

The last weekend of April, we were ready to plant the seedlings—an entire month earlier than the year before. I could hardly believe it! And these weren't the frail little wimpy seedlings of year one. These were basement-bred warriors ready to take root in their new outdoor home. Their roots had grit, and their stems had backbone.

Not only that, the compost finally broke down enough to have that sweet-spot texture—dark and grippy, like brownie crumbs on a good day. Thanks to my diligence in the hardening-off process (a phrase that still sounds like I'm prepping my plants for emotional warfare), the seedlings weren't the least bit fazed by the wind, sun, or life outside the glow of grow lights. There would be significantly less stress after the transplant this year. Progress.

My husband worked so hard to get the new drip irrigation system in place, and it was incredible. I knew these seedlings would be served better by getting water directly at the soil level, hoping it would keep powdery mildew and disease at bay. What I didn't expect was how much the irrigation lines would lead me to be a bit more orderly in my planting. The shape of the overall garden might still have been a triangle. Yet, the deliberate positioning of seedlings along the irrigation lines shifted my very avant-garde approach from the prior year, giving the garden a much more intentional feel.

As the saying goes, however, one step forward, two steps back. Just as I was feeling proud of how structured my second-year garden bed looked, dozens of volunteer plants from the year before started popping up, in places I never planted them, and in numbers I definitely didn't sign off on. The Bells of Ireland had reseeded themselves and not only reappeared unexpectedly, but multiplied and spread far beyond last season's borders. Thankfully, they were also thriving in ways they hadn't before. The problem? They weren't in neat, tidy rows like everything else I'd just planted—and many quickly crowded out seedlings I thought would have plenty of room.

The "magic celosia" in my front beds years ago was nothing compared to its encore performance in the cut flower garden. There, the celosia came back with a vengeance—and a sassy little attitude. Maybe it was the lack of mulch, which had suppressed some of the growth out front. Or maybe it was the fish emulsion I was already faithfully applying. Whatever the cause, in the spot where I had tucked in about 20 basement-grown seedlings, there were now *hundreds* of volunteers all competing for space. Apparently, I didn't need to start celosia ever again—they self-seeded *just fine*.

I was quickly reminded of how little control I really had. I'm convinced Mother Nature is an Enneagram 8—strong-willed, unbothered, and definitely not taking orders from me. It was like she was saying, "Thanks for all your little trays and your fish fertilizer, but I'll take it from here."

It was humbling—and also, kind of amazing. Because as chaotic as it felt to watch things pop up wherever they pleased, the truth was—it was working. These weren't weak, struggling plants. These were thriving, bold, wildly successful surprises. While I had mapped the garden like a blueprint, she scribbled outside every line. Though my inner control freak was twitching at the lack of order, my heart was lighting up at the sheer abundance of it all.

Somewhere between "this isn't what I planned" and "this is actually better," I felt a softening in myself. I was being reminded—again—that surrender isn't the opposite of effort, it's part of it.

As I watched so much come to life beyond what I had planned, I was struck by the potential inside a single, solitary seed. Have you ever seen how tiny a celosia seed is? It's no bigger than a poppy seed—maybe even smaller. You tuck it into a seed tray in midwinter, water and feed it, tend to it until it's ready for the outdoors. Then, after a little growth outside, you pinch it—and somehow that little act prompts it to multiply its branching. By the heat of summer, you're standing there surrounded by plushy plumes in the most stunning array of colors, many of them taller than you.

What's astounding is that each of those plumes produces literally hundreds of seeds. One plant can hold dozens of plumes—so a single seed can multiply into thousands more. From one tiny, almost insignificant-looking speck, you could harvest enough seed to fill acres of space ... which would then produce *trillions* more. The same is true for zinnias, dahlias, cosmos, gomphrena, and marigolds—just to name a few. Each one is, in its own way, a little overachiever.

I think about how effortless this all seems in nature, and I can't help but compare it to other parts of my life. Remember that weekend I decided to bake 27 loaves of banana bread for all my new college friends? Not effortless. The time we bought an outdated A-frame, hoping it would become an income-producing rental? Definitely not effortless. All the theme parties I threw in my 30s? Fun, yes—but a whole lot of work.

The mystery of what can spring from a single seed makes me pause and consider a different kind of reality—one I believe reflects the abundant, generous, elaborate love of God. A love that reminds me of how good and beauty can break through at any time, despite—and apart from—any effort of my own.

I need this reminder in my life—that I'm not solely responsible for creating good and beauty in the world. I want to be a co-creator, yes. But I also need to remember—often—that goodness and beauty can arrive without any effort of my own. And not just quietly, but extravagantly. Uncontrollably. In ways that spill over my carefully laid plans and grow into something far better than I dared hope for.

There's something sacred about the relationship between the one who plants a seed and the God who makes it grow. Any gardening—any act of creating, really—is a partnership that requires both effort and surrender. Through my (admittedly limited) experience with hands in the soil, I've come to believe this partnership is not only welcomed by God but deeply desired. We were never meant to do it all alone. I think the Divine delights in working alongside and through us. Beauty isn't just something we produce after all—it's something we also embody.

Of course, this goes far beyond gardening. This partnership shows up in writing music, creating art, raising children, comforting a friend, building something from scratch, and in infinite acts of co-creation. Some say it all comes from within, but every time I tend seeds and give what I can to help them grow, I'm reminded: It doesn't all rest on me. I'm simply invited into the process. And in that co-creation, my heart expands. I begin to see—just a little more—how wildly and generously God multiplies even the smallest efforts.

Maybe that's the most comforting truth of all: I don't have to force beauty. I don't even have to earn it. I just have to make space for it.

And that understanding makes me want to keep giving, keep planting, keep showing up in other corners of life with open hands, trusting that God can do so much ... with so very little.

You can plan for order. You can work hard. You can show up every day. But sometimes the best thing you grow is the thing you never planted—

The grace that surprises you.
The joy that finds you.
The beauty that keeps on multiplying long after your hands let go.

CHAPTER TWENTY-ONE

RIP IT FROM THE ROOT

The only thing more prolific than the self-seeded celosia in our garden that second summer were the weeds. I thought I'd had a lot the first year, pulling them up every weekend like a dutiful suburban gardening heroine. But in 2024? Well, you'd swear weeds were the star crop I'd been cultivating all along. I even flirted with making a cute, Etsy-worthy sign for the gate that read, *Welcome to My Weed Garden.* Then I paused—because let's be real, that might send some super mixed messages about what kind of "weed" I was actually growing. And after our hydroponics store debut, let's just say I didn't need any more rumors.

Since I'm committed to doing this whole "suburban micro flower farm" thing 100% organically, I don't use any weed killers. Even if I weren't so crunchy about it, I'd still hesitate—because the weeds are usually so deeply intertwined with the good stuff, pulling one out sometimes feels like tugging on a thread and unraveling the whole sweater. This is a whole different beast compared to my landscaping beds, which have had years of love, layers of weed barrier, and mulch so thick it could muffle Bon Jovi belting out 'Livin' on a Prayer' at full volume. Sure, a few weeds sneak through there, but nothing like the jungle I'm wrangling in the cut flower bed.

So, a couple times a week, armed with an audiobook and a paper grocery bag, I set out to handpick weeds from the roots—because anything less feels like a band-aid on a broken bone. I've tried every weed-removing tool known to gardeners. Spoiler alert: Most of them double as weapons of mass irrigation tape destruction. They're designed to be razor sharp to slice weeds just below the soil, but with our lines spaced every 12 inches, they're nearly impossible to avoid. Plus, the weeds somehow always manage to grow right underneath the irrigation line to the point I'm pretty confident they've entered into a full-blown alliance with Satan himself.

While I appreciate the moments I can whack a weed with a hoe or wield my Hori Hori knife like a garden ninja, sometimes it's just easier (and oddly satisfying) to pull everything out by hand.

"But what about weed barrier?" you ask. Sure, it sounds like the obvious answer—but (old news) I'm stubborn. It's not just that I dislike how it looks when it's not covered by mulch. I also go pseudo-hippie in my hope of avoiding plastic. (We've already established that I do everything the hard way. Thanks for loving me anyway.) Yes, some barriers claim to biodegrade, but I live in a subdivision. All I can picture is tiny bits of weed-barrier confetti blowing into my neighbors' yards like sad, unwanted party favors, which is not exactly the vibe I'm going for, thanks.

So I settle into the slow, patient work of hand-pulling, one root at a time. It's meditative in that "this might never end, but I'm trying to grow as a person" kind of way. Sometimes I think of it like editing a messy draft—removing what doesn't belong so the real story can shine through. Only this version includes dirt under your fingernails and the occasional spider sprinting up your arm just to keep things spicy.

Here's what I find myself thinking about when I pull those little baby weeds out one by one: I envision the beauty that's coming from the seeds I've carefully tended. I picture the roots they're establishing and the blooms they want to produce. I think about the space they need to thrive and the nutrients they need from the soil. Then, I intervene on their behalf—weed by weed—pulling out what doesn't belong so they can get on with the business of blooming.

It's not by accident that weeds often grow right next to what you're trying to cultivate. They need sunlight, water, and nutrients just like flowers do. When you start adding compost, fertilizing, and providing the perfect conditions for growth, you might as well send out party invitations to every dormant weed seed in the ZIP code. Turns out they were always there, just waiting for your good intentions to wake them up so the party could start.

Not only that, but they seem to grow faster and easier than the things you're trying to nurture. Weeds are the hustlers of the plant world. They spread fast, don't wait for permission, and roll into your garden like they own the place—no RSVP, no manners, just a pocket full of bad intentions and the gall to call it confidence.

Cut them back, pull them out, and somehow they will still find a way to return—sometimes from just a sliver of root. There's something admirable in that kind of persistence. Something defiant and quietly noble. It reminds us to keep showing up, even when life tries to bury us. Even when we've been broken down to almost nothing, there's still something in us—hope, grit, maybe a little fierce stubbornness—that pushes through the dirt and reaches for the light. It's not pretty or poetic, but it's real—and sometimes, that's enough to start again.

As much as I admire that scrappy spirit, let's be clear: Weeds make terrible roommates. They don't just grow—they crowd and invade. They barrel through boundaries, muscle into the sunlight, and hijack every ounce of water and nutrients without so much as a thank-you. Their goal isn't coexistence—it's dominance. Left unchecked, they will choke the life out of anything softer, slower, or still finding its footing. It's a power grab, plain and simple. And unless you intervene, they'll win.

That's the thing about invaders—they don't need your permission, just your absence. And if you're not paying attention, they'll take root in places that were never meant for them. So while I can respect the sheer audacity of a weed, I've also learned that unchecked growth is not the same as thriving. Some things flourish by force, not by purpose. Which is why not everything that grows deserves to stay. Not every yes is meant for you. Not every opportunity is aligned with your purpose. So we learn to pull what doesn't belong—habits that drain us, expectations we never agreed to, fears disguised as practicality—before they settle in and think they own the place.

It's a bit like life, isn't it? There's always something loud and fast-growing trying to edge out the quiet, tender things you've been patiently nurturing—your peace, your purpose, your late-in-the-day exhale. And just like in the garden, it's up to us to notice—to kneel down into the dirt of our days and ask, "Is this helping me grow, or is it just taking up space?"

I've only recently turned 50 and have finally figured out how to weed out what doesn't belong in my life—chaos, comparison, my own self-criticism, people who take more than they give, or a quick yes that becomes its own version of a shiny trap. They're all weeds threatening to keep me from blooming into the best version of myself. It took a while, but I get it now. I have to pull these weeds—sometimes over and over again—and I have to rip them out from the root. It would be tragic to let them choke out the beauty that's meant to grow in and around me.

I'm done babysitting weeds that were never mine to grow. These days, I rip them out—expectations I never agreed to, comparisons I didn't sign up for, chaos I never invited. I guard my peace like treasure and even build small fences around my sanity if I have to. And I'll keep pulling until the roots let go.

Weed the garden of your life with savage conviction.
Beauty shouldn't have to beg for space.
Neither should you.

CHAPTER TWENTY-TWO

NOT EVERYTHING
THAT GROWS BELONGS

I've mentioned that my husband is an architect. What I *haven't* told you is that he somehow managed to turn me—a deeply committed, color-worshiping maximalist—into a woman who now uses the word *edit* without gagging.

When we fell in love as grown adults, we suddenly found ourselves with two homes and one life to blend. For the sheer goodness of having a second bathroom—and probably equally for the serenity of a quieter street—we sold his place and moved into mine. I'd lived there for a decade, but I wanted it to feel like *ours* from the moment he and the boys moved in. So I started asking Jeremy what he envisioned for the space.

Now, you need to know something about me: I have this strange superpower for noticing undertones in color. I'll catch the whisper of green in brown, or know instantly when a white is leaning yellow. I don't just like color—I feel it. Which probably explains why, over the course of a decade, my house morphed into a live-in color wheel.

At one point, someone called it "The Skittles House." Not because it was loud—but because every room had its own meticulously selected vibe: terracotta, brick red, smoky blue, that moody green-gray sky color that rolls in before a Midwest thunderstorm. Each space flowed into the next, tied together by a shared saturation. Pops of complementary color anchored every room—the burnt orange pillows against the smoky blue walls of the living room with its quirky green lamp in the corner. The brick-red kitchen glowing with thrifted colored glass lit softly by string lights. Everything had a place. Every piece had a story. It was layered and warm and full of life, and I spent *ten years* perfecting every nook accordingly.

But then he said *the words*. The words no color-lover wants to hear:

"I've always dreamed of an all-white house."

And I, in return, dreamed of faking my own death.

I truly wanted Jeremy and the boys to move in and feel at home. So when Jeremy told me his dream was an all-white house, I smiled and nodded like a supportive partner while internally wondering if we were about to turn my beloved home into a sterile dental office. He explained that white gives art the chance to breathe. That editing—or paring down—makes space for what truly matters to sing. I silently reminded myself that I'd promised to make this space *ours*, not just mine. So I said, bravely, "Let's do it," and waved goodbye to the perfectly muted rainbow world I had so lovingly built.

A few weeks later, after every wall, ceiling, and bit of trim had been coated in the crispest, purest white we could find, Jeremy came home from work. He walked in, took one look around, and said with absolute sincerity, "This doesn't work, does it?" I breathed the biggest sigh of relief, blurting "I hate it!" through grateful laughter once I knew we were on the same page.

And just like that, we began again—together.

We painted a focal wall black. He designed a sleek wooden installation to replace the old fireplace, with a clean-lined niche that doubled as a modern mantle for our Christmas stockings. Slowly, we started layering warmth back in. The white was still there, but it had something to lean on. The cold edges softened. The space began to feel like us—a little him, a little me, a whole lot of creativity bouncing back and forth between the two of us.

I love modern design. I might always swoon over architectural flourishes and antiques with chipped paint and mysterious past lives, but Jeremy has helped me see both the beauty in restraint and the boldness of simplicity.

But my garden? Oh, my garden was where I planned to let my inner maximalist out without apology.

At least, that's what I expected.

In my second year of gardening, I went feral. Why grow four types of zinnias when you can grow twelve? Why stop at cosmos when you can try lisianthus, craspedia, asters, and heirloom chrysanthemums? When Floret released their first line of celosia and zinnia seeds, you better believe I wanted to grow *every single one.* So I did. By mid-July, the garden looked like a jungle, risking HOA fines—gorgeous, yes, but so stuffed with possibility that there was barely room to walk.

That's when something surprising happened.

As the season went on, I found myself walking through that crazy, overflowing plot the way I walk through my house now. I spotted what wasn't working, noticed what wasn't thriving, and called out what was quietly stealing light from what I really wanted to flourish. And I began to edit. Not just the weeds, but the good stuff, too—the self-seeded volunteers, the pretty-but-meh plants I'd overhyped in my mind. Even the ones I'd babied like newborns the summer before, I yanked without blinking if they were crowding out something better.

It's a strange kind of pruning—removing not just the weeds, but the good things that no longer belong. The extras that are lovely but no longer purposeful. It's editing the garden not because it wasn't beautiful, but because you're trying to make space for the beauty that *deserves* to grow.

That's where I find myself lately—not just with flowers, but with life. Sifting through the loud and the lovely, the wild and the worthy. Pulling what chokes, clearing what clutters, and learning—slowly—that sometimes growth looks like less. Sometimes it looks like saying no to something beautiful so that something *essential* has room to breathe.

That's when I realized gardening isn't just a wild, throw-everything-in-and-hope-for-the-best kind of art. It's like designing a room. Or telling a story. Sometimes you have to let go of something beautiful so something *essential* can flourish. Sometimes the editing—the subtracting—is the thing that brings clarity.

Life often starts the same way: with a full heart, full hands, full schedule, full inbox. You gather. You grow. You say yes. And it's beautiful—until it's not. Until the thing that once brought joy starts choking out your peace. You realize that maybe more *isn't* more. That maybe growth means gently pulling something out—*even something good*—so that the things that matter most have the room they need to bloom.

We start out wanting it all—more plans, more clothes, more blooms, more experiences. So we fill every inch of our time, our closets, and our garden beds. We say yes to everything because it all feels important, urgent, beautiful, and even necessary. We confuse fullness with flourishing. And in the beginning, maybe we actually *need* the untamed, overgrown season to help us discover what we actually love.

But if we're paying attention—and willing to do the unglamorous work of reflection—we start to notice what's crowding out the light. What's thriving and what's just surviving. What's bringing joy and what's draining it.

Whether you're decorating a room, building a life, or tending a plot of land, editing isn't about loss. It's about clarity, focus, and grace.

And then comes the harder part: letting go. Not out of scarcity, but from a deeper knowing—a confidence that not every good thing is the right thing. That space is not waste; it's possibility. That boundaries aren't barriers; they're trellises for growth.

We stop clinging to what once made sense and start making space for what fits now. We edit—not to erase, but to refine and to reveal.

We remove what's merely "fine" so what's meaningful can take root. We say no to the almost-right so we can say yes to what is absolutely, undeniably right for us.

Whether it's a flower bed, a living room, a friendship, a dream, or a Thursday afternoon—you get to shape it. You get to tend it. You get to ask: *Is this helping me bloom?* And if the answer is no, you get to pull it out—even if it was once, or even still is, beautiful.

Because editing isn't just a creative act.
It's a courageous one.

And much like any good garden, a good life needs space for the light to get in.

CHAPTER TWENTY-THREE

LEGACY IN BLOOM

There's a rather epic photo of me on the first day of a new year in high school, standing by the front door in an outfit I literally sewed myself. It was … special. I think in the late 1980s/early 90s, whatever I was wearing was called a "jumper." Consider what might happen if a pair of overalls and an empire-waisted maxi dress had a baby. Now picture it in a floral print, giving strong curtains vibes; though I would argue today it would have been *a lot* even for curtains.

Now picture a matching bow for my hot-roller-curled hair, all pulled into a side ponytail, except for my massive bangs. I mean, clearly what I needed in this scenario was a matching hair accessory. And the cherry on top? A pair of fake eyeglasses from Claire's. Did I need glasses? Nope. But I was convinced my outfit wouldn't have been complete without them—and I have always been unapologetically me. I like to think I have aged like a fine wine, only getting better and more sophisticated with time, but I'm probably still the same dork I've always been, who thinks I'm way cooler than I actually am. C'est la vie.

The full, awkward glory of me during my teen years still lives within me now, even at the ripe age of 50, no matter how well she may or may not have improved and evolved with time. So when I sing my pretty song about editing, I need to also be fully transparent. While I was getting better about ripping out what didn't belong in my cut flower garden, I simultaneously decided to both start a vegetable garden *and* develop a new area in a completely different part of our backyard, which I affectionately called "The Annex."

What's The Annex, you ask? Well, it *was* a 5x10-foot bare patch along a fence on the north side of our backyard begging for some attention. The grass wasn't growing well anyway, so I naturally thought to throw down a couple bags of compost, till it in with the dirt, and plant a bunch of zinnia and sunflower seeds. Because heaven forbid you waste any space whatsoever. I mean, show me a gardener with enough space, and I'll show you a unicorn riding a tractor.

And so The Annex was born. With a few seeds still left to plant and enough chicken wire to fend off rabbits, I thought, *why not?* I can now tell you why not: no irrigation line, not enough light, and poor soil. Nothing much came of it, but you can't blame a girl for trying. Besides, I hope I'll always be the one who looks at bare dirt and thinks, *I bet something beautiful could grow here.*

I firmly believe most everything has a lesson in it somewhere to learn, so after reflecting a bit on why I even started The Annex in the first place, I decided I actually *did* want more space to grow cut flowers— I just didn't want them to be so far from the rest of the garden. And thus, plans began to form for a 2025 garden expansion. Did I tell Jeremy? Not yet, but my brain was noodling the idea and trying to figure out how it would all work.

At the same time The Annex was going in, Jeremy pitched the idea of a vegetable garden. Because nothing says romance like crop rotation, I was quickly starting vegetable seeds in our basement between trays of flowers. When he suggested growing a few things we could actually eat and not just look at, the answer was a clear and resounding yes. Bonus points that it might also keep us alive in case of an apocalypse.

Jeremy spent much of his childhood with his grandparents, who kept a big vegetable garden in their backyard. For him, the idea of growing vegetables again carried a sense of nostalgia. Interestingly, it was his stories about their garden that stirred my own memories of how much my grandma loved flowers. Listening to him talk transported me back to her backyard, filled with roses and irises in bloom. As a kid, though, I mostly found it annoying when she insisted on walking me and my sisters around to see every plant—because <ahem> she also had a pool. A 10-year-old can only feign so much enthusiasm for rose petals when the water is calling.

Looking back, I wonder if she's the one who originally planted this seed in me—if my passion for flowers was quietly rooted in those childhood walks through her garden. Maybe Jeremy's longing to grow vegetables came from the hours he once spent with his Papa amongst the rows. Whatever the reason, I found myself growing tomatoes and peppers with him simply because he wanted to—and maybe, just maybe, I started dreaming of planting iris bulbs that fall.

When Jeremy and I got married in our late 30s, we had seven living grandparents. S-E-V-E-N. Except for my dad's mom, who sadly passed away before I was born, every one of them was miraculously still with us. We knew how extraordinary that was and never took it for granted. Now, twelve years later, we've said goodbye to all of them—but we've also found small, meaningful ways to keep them close.

Jeremy's Papa not only loved his garden—he also adored Dolly Parton. Which is why, yes, we now have Papa's beloved Dolly Parton trash can in our primary bedroom. Do I laugh almost every time I see it? Absolutely. His Meme taught me how to make her famous chocolate gravy—Jeremy's most requested birthday and holiday treat. Do I feel like I'm slowly killing him every time I whip up a batch? Absolutely, positively yes.

It's funny how seemingly insignificant things can keep you connected to the people you've lost. For us, vegetable gardening became part of that thread. The deer may have quickly devoured our pepper plants (annoying), but we still managed to grow several tomato plants from seed and ate cherry tomatoes straight off the vine like candy. Honestly, nothing compares to a sun-warmed, homegrown tomato in the middle of summer.

Several times that summer, I watched Jeremy tending our little vegetable patch and imagined him as a boy in his Papa's garden on hot Oklahoma days, the sun catching his very blonde hair. I pictured the two of them laughing together—Papa in his striped overalls, Jeremy flashing that sweet, perfect smile. It must have felt like heaven on earth. Probably some of the best days not only for Jeremy, but for his grandparents, too.

Surprisingly, I found myself wondering if one day we might have grandkids who will also spend time with us in the garden as they grow up. Maybe David will have a little boy who eats tomatoes off the vine with Jeremy, juice and seeds dripping down his cute little chin. Maybe JJ will have a little girl whose blue eyes sparkle as she plays hide-and-seek with me among the flowers. It's wild to think that what we're cultivating now could plant the same sense of wonder and magic in them that Jeremy found in his Papa's garden—or that I first discovered walking through my grandma's roses.

I didn't start into vegetable gardening because I thought I'd love it. I did it because I knew Jeremy would. But somewhere along the way, I realized this: Sometimes you put your hands to something, and it quietly does holy work in the background. While the flowers sparked creativity, the vegetables sparked connection. Suddenly, the whole thing carried weight—significance, purpose, and even the hope of legacy.

With every bouquet I dropped off with friends and every daydream of what might come someday, I started to grasp how gardening spreads joy like celosia spreads seed. It carries so much further beyond what you intended originally, it invades spaces you didn't expect, and it can do so for generations to come.

So I allowed myself to dream even bigger dreams for not only our cut flower garden and our new vegetable patch, but also about what this whole space could become. Could we make our yard a place of wild, abundant beauty—not simply for us? Could it also become a beautiful, playful place our grandkids would one day grow up remembering? Could it be a backdrop for their childhood magic? Could it become the kind of place where seeds of joy, peace, and wonder take root?

Because here's what I'm learning: Sometimes growth isn't simply happening in the garden bed. Many times, it's also in the dream that comes next.

It's in the glimpse of what this space might become—not just for me, but for the people who will walk it long after I'm gone. It's in the hope that roots planted now will outlast my own hands in the soil. It's in the dream that stretches past today's blooms into a legacy of beauty, joy, and wonder.

The Annex didn't work—but it taught me that I really wanted more space to grow things. The idea of the vegetable garden didn't originally thrill me—but it connected me to love and memory. And all of it, even the messy middle, made me dream a little deeper about what's possible.

Growth doesn't always look like blossoms. Sometimes it looks like plans on paper, or a conversation under string lights, or a hand reaching for a seed you're not quite ready to plant. Sometimes, the richest roots are the ones you can't yet see. And maybe that's the point—because legacy isn't just what you grow, it's what you set in motion for someone else.

So I will keep dreaming about and planning out new corners of the garden and noodling on what comes next. Because even when something doesn't grow, it can still plant the dream that will. Maybe that's the real legacy of a garden—it teaches us that even the smallest seeds, the smallest gestures, can outlast us in ways we may never see.

CHAPTER TWENTY-FOUR

THE FOURTH DIMENSION

When we were prepping Jeremy's house to sell back when we were engaged, the buyers wanted insulation of a certain rating to be put in the attic. It was the absolute peak heat of the summer, and though we could have hired it out, Jeremy and I have always been DIY-ers. He firmly believes you can learn how to do anything by watching enough YouTube videos (he's right!), so we've done big things like building our own deck and renovating an A-frame, and small things like replacing garbage disposals and, well … installing new attic insulation.

Thankfully, the home wasn't huge, so it wasn't a massive project. Serendipitously, we discovered a massive Menards sale on rolled insulation the next weekend. Jeremy did some rough math and determined how many rolls we would need, then we hopped in his Chevy HHR and headed an hour north to the closest Menards (the only one in the Kansas City area at the time).

Anyone who knows what a Chevy HHR is knows a) it's clearly the absolute sexiest car an eligible bachelor could ever drive and b) it most definitely would not hold the amount of insulation Jeremy intended to stuff inside. He knew I absolutely did *not* believe in the feasibility of this mission. So when we got to Menards and bought the insulation, I stood by his car and said, "I can't wait to watch you try to do this," as he started to load the rolls in the back.

Did they all fit? Absolutely not. Did he decide the next right step would be to strap them on the roof? You betcha. So, back inside Menards he went to get rolls of packing film and rope, because let's also clarify there was no roof rack on his vehicle. Sure enough, when all was said and done, he somehow managed to get all of the insulation in or *on* his car. He full on MacGyvered that insulation like it was a high-stakes game of adult Tetris.

We laughed the whole way home (going 35 mph max) so much my sides hurt the next day. Even then, we knew it would be a memory that brought repeated smiles over the course of our life together. I have poked fun at Jeremy for a decade at how much he thought would fit *inside* his HHR, as well as how much he was able to fit *on* his HHR. But one must be careful about what one says, because goodness gracious, those words can sure come back to bite you later.

My garden? It's basically the botanical equivalent of Jeremy's insulation-stuffed car.

I hear him poke fun at me every time seeds show up in the mail. "Where exactly are these going?" he asks, knowing the garden is already well beyond capacity. And though I could reply, "On the roof of your old HHR," I smile instead and say, "I'll figure it out."

At this point, you know I bought way more seeds for 2024 than I could have possibly used. I'm probably set until 2027—or even longer. So when I found out I could also buy "plugs" of some flowers I wanted to try but had been too late in getting going for the 2024 season, of course I ordered some. Because if I don't have room for all the seeds, clearly what I needed was *more live plants*.

Plugs are seedlings started by other farmers and sold to folks who don't have the space, the time, the desire, or the sanity—to grow their own from scratch. They're especially helpful with finicky varieties. For my second summer, I had my heart set on lisianthus, which everyone warned me were among the trickiest seeds to start and grow well.

Entire Facebook groups exist just to help gardeners troubleshoot their struggles, and one glance at a thread was enough to convince me to heed the advice repeated over and over: *Just buy plugs.* A quick Google search led me to Etsy sellers offering them in small quantities, so I picked three colors for that first year and anxiously awaited their arrival.

I had to rip a few things out to make space for them, and I was probably planting them a bit late since lisianthus is considered a cool-season flower. I kept seeing people talk about cool-season flowers (aka hardy annuals) versus warm-season annuals, but I didn't really understand the difference. A flower-farmer friend suggested I pick up the book *"Cool Flowers"* by Lisa Mason Ziegler, which led me to her online course—and that, in turn, unlocked for me a whole new level of crazy.

Suddenly, everything I thought I knew about timing and planting was upended. Growing up in Kansas City, I always heard you shouldn't plant annuals outside until Mother's Day—when the risk of frost had passed and the soil was finally warm enough to help things grow. But Lisa was teaching something completely different: that some annual flowers actually preferred being planted in the fall so they could "overwinter," and that certain seeds needed to be sown *before* the ground froze in order to undergo a period of "cold stratification."

This new-to-me tidbit blew my mind! I finally understood why my poppy crop had failed for two years: They didn't like growing when it was warm. Also, in order for my ranunculus to really have a shot, they needed to be in the ground in late February or early March, with frost cloth on standby if needed. Suddenly, this whole gardening game was less of a sprint to Mother's Day and more like a four-dimensional chess match with time.

I would need a calendar and a well-planned strategy. A seasonal version of the site plan Jeremy had drawn up for me—one that showed what would be pulled out when, and what could be planted next. When the ranunculus finished blooming, I could plant dahlias in their place. After the larkspur faded, I could sow zinnias. Maybe I could actually use all those seeds I bought! Maybe the plugs I ordered could shine for a season, then make way for something new. Suddenly, my garden wasn't limited. It was an invitation to grow in succession.

The plot thickened. Literally.

So there I was, in the heat of summer, already planning for winter. Plotting my poppy comeback. Strategizing sweet peas. Making room for lisianthus. Dreaming of anemones and delphinium. It was on like Donkey Kong, and I was up for the challenge.

What started as a scramble to keep plants alive had become strategy, rhythm, and long-game thinking. The more I mapped out, the more I realized gardening wasn't just about today's blooms—it was about creating room for what came next.

Gardening, much like life, isn't just about what grows *now*. It's about planting into the possibility of *next*. I used to think gardening was all about one big planting weekend in May. One chance, one window, one shot—but now I see it's about rhythms, seasons, and cycles. The layering of beauty across time.

The garden taught me about the fourth dimension—that time itself is a tool. Blooming isn't just about what's visible today. It's about what's been buried, nurtured, and tended across time. It's about knowing some things won't flower for months, but you plant them anyway. Because even though the dirt looks quiet, something is stirring— something is preparing. Just because you don't see it yet doesn't mean it isn't happening.

Maybe that's the real invitation: to remember that not every season is meant for blooming. Some are for rooting, for resting, for holding space while the magic does its quiet work underground. Some chapters in life look dormant on the surface, but underneath, everything is shifting. Growth doesn't always demand urgency. Sometimes it's about soft soil, open hands, and faith in what's unseen. And sometimes it's about planting seeds for the version of yourself you haven't even met yet.

And that, much like a Chevy HHR full of insulation, you're capable of holding a whole lot more potential than most anyone gives you credit for—even if you have to strap it to the roof and take the long way home, laughing all the way, knowing you just planted something you'll likely never forget.

CHAPTER TWENTY-FIVE

SEED. FAIL. REPEAT.

They say if you ever need it to rain, just wash your car. In my case? Plant cosmos seeds. Every single time I tried in 2024, the forecasted "slight chance of showers" turned into a full-blown flash flood. Not once, not twice—close to half a dozen times. I couldn't make this up if I tried.

Planting right before a gentle rain? Ideal. Planting right before your yard morphs into the neighborhood storm drain? Not so much. Each downpour turned my flower beds into a rushing river, carrying those poor cosmos halfway to the fence before the clouds even cleared. I'd sit inside, listening to the deluge pound the roof, knowing my freshly sown seeds were floating into oblivion. And every time, I'd sigh and add "buy more cosmos seeds" to the errand list like it was some kind of cosmic joke.

The weather in May of 2024 was, in a word, rude. While I was busy planting and replanting cosmos like a woman trying to outwit fate, I was also waiting for a dry window to get my dahlia tubers in the ground. You might recall I'd tried a few the year before—treating them like they were spun sugar and unicorn hair at every turn—only to discover, once they finally bloomed, that I'd been sent the wrong ones. Lovely? Sure. What I ordered and hoped for? Not even close. So for year two, I wised up and ordered from small family farms with reputations for sending what you pay for. Revolutionary, I know.

When the rain finally let up, I tucked 15 different varieties of dahlia tubers (because of course I did) into the garden—along with yet another round of cosmos seeds (bless). Ironically, even without flash flooding, the cosmos staged a protest that year. They showed up late, sulked at half their usual height, and basically phoned it in like flowers on strike.

But the dahlias? Oh, the dahlias won my heart that year. I was completely captivated by their beauty—awestruck as they unfurled layer after layer, to the point I didn't even care about the cosmos.

That summer, I pulled out every trick in my organic gardening toolbelt to protect what I could. I even learned about protecting dahlia blooms with organza bags, cinching them closed around the stem to keep out cucumber beetles and other tiny garden gremlins in search of a snack.

But by mid-July, after weeks of wet heat that felt like gardening inside Satan's armpit, powdery mildew showed up two months earlier than the year before and took the zinnias down. I tried everything, and still lost the battle. Plants were yanked out long before their time in a desperate attempt to save the rest of the garden. Miraculously, the dahlias stood strong. They held out until the very end, bowing only when the first frost finally called the season closed.

It was wild to witness how the same plot of land could yield such different stories depending on that particular season's weather. It affected everything from pests and disease, to bloom size and plant health. Once again, none of which I could control. At this point, I knew I was but a supporting actor to Mother Nature, filling in gaps where heat or drought left scars—and cleaning up the mess after surprise windstorms or an unsolicited rainstorm. While some plants thrived, others crumbled. Some bloomed beyond expectation. Others ghosted me like a bad online date.

When a patch of flowers you've nurtured from seed, corm, bulb, or tuber succumbs to weather or disease before its time, it's a gut punch. Every early exit carried away not only the blooms but also my carefully laid plans for how I hoped to share them. I wanted to bless so many people with their beauty—and yet, there was nothing I could do to save them.

Gardening doesn't just teach patience; it also teaches resilience. The kind that rolls up its sleeves, gets muddy, and shows up even when discouraged. The kind that buys more cosmos seed for the sixth time because maybe—just maybe—*this* time will be different.

It's heartbreaking to pull up something you've nurtured from nothing. To rip out dreams mid-bloom. But resilience isn't measured by what survives—it's measured by the willingness to try again, even while your heart is still nursing disappointment. It isn't loud or flashy. It's quiet and gritty. It's a tender, repeated yes.

To put it simply, to be resilient is to *keep showing up*—even when the weather mocks your best efforts, or your carefully laid plans get upstaged by powdery mildew. It's learning to bless what *did* grow, even when what you *hoped* for didn't. It's the courage to try new methods, new timing, new tubers—even after you got burned the first (or second or third) time.

It means we keep sowing beauty into the world, even when we're not sure what will come of it. But somehow—miraculously—something always does.

It's easy to show up when everything goes according to plan. It's another thing entirely to keep showing up when everything goes sideways. But that's what gardeners do. We roll up our sleeves and try again. Because somewhere beneath the mess, the mildew, and the misfires, there's still beauty fighting to bloom—and I'm not about to miss it.

That's the lesson the garden keeps whispering to me: It's always worth it to try again. Beauty still belongs to those who don't give up—who kneel down in the dirt, muddy-kneed and open-hearted, believing something good can still take root. The garden doesn't reward perfection. It honors persistence. And it will meet you—cosmos seed packet in hand—right in the middle of your imperfect, overwatered, beautifully hopeful mess.

Because life is surely going to be a mess at times, but it might as well be a blooming one.

CHAPTER TWENTY-SIX

LET BEAUTY LEAD

What do you gain after all the sweat, the digging, the weed-pulling, the fertilizing, the pinching, the watering, the endless sunscreen reapplying, the Japanese-beetle-into-soapy-water-flicking, and the baby-bunny outwitting? For some, a garden. For me? It's the creativity that blooms right alongside the flowers—the joy of arranging them after months of gritty work. That's truly what fuels my stubborn commitment to the whole process. Because when it's all said and done, the deepest joy of this suburban micro flower farm isn't just watching things grow. It's the moment I finally get to place stems one by one, intentionally and artistically displaying their beauty in bloom.

Could I just go buy flowers? Of course. That would be infinitely simpler. But there's something incredible about nurturing a seed into bloom and then getting to design with it—that's where the real wonder lives for me. The magic doubles when I cut, arrange, and create with the fruits of my own labor. It's a unique kind of satisfaction to be part of the process from the first tiny seed to the final arrangement on a table.

Something in me wakes up—at the deepest soul level—when I get to play with shape, color, and scale. Taking what I've grown and designing something that brings sunshine indoors and sparks joy every time it's seen. All those years of art training and decades as a creative suddenly find a place to land, as I curate blooms to complement one another. It has become the most unexpected love in this second half of my life. Honestly, I could play with flowers all day, every day, and be the happiest woman alive.

What I've learned over the last few years is that the best arrangements—much like the best seasons in life—are all about balance. Not perfection. Not symmetry. Balance. Imperfection matters because you need contrast and a little tension to make things interesting. Asymmetry matters because something tall, curly, or downright weird poking out says, "Hey there. Didn't expect me, did you? But look—I belong here, too." The unexpected doesn't just belong—it's often the very thing that turns ordinary into extraordinary. Nature itself is wild and untamed, constantly reminding us that beauty shows up in the most unlikely places.

Every good arrangement needs scale and variety: big blooms to catch your eye, airy sprigs to add movement, sturdy stems to hold it all together. You need texture *and* blank space. Drama *and* calm. The same goes for life. The loud, dazzling moments are fun, but without the pauses in between, we run ourselves straight into adrenal collapse. We desperately need negative space—those open, unfilled gaps that let the rest of who we are breathe. A life jammed edge to edge without any white space may look full, but it won't *feel* beautiful. It will feel overwhelming, even crushing. (Ask anyone who's ever overbooked themselves and ended up sobbing in their car in the Target parking lot. Hypothetically speaking, of course.)

Balance doesn't mean equal parts, either. Sometimes you need one dahlia and three sprigs of basil. A few rudbeckias and even more astilbe. Sometimes you need one predominant voice in a quiet room—or a quiet moment in the middle of chaos. Sometimes you need a season of adventure followed by a long winter's nap. Sometimes you just need to take a walk by yourself because you've had enough people-ing. Sometimes you need an ice cream cone after seven days of eating according to plan. Balance reveals what to add, what to soften, and when to let something wild hang out the side just because it makes you smile.

When arranging flowers, it's easy to think beauty is just about what's visible—the finished arrangement, the highlight reel—not the behind-the-scenes. However, anyone who's arranged flowers knows that's only half the story. It's the unseen work that matters most.

The secret to making something shine isn't just what you add; it's how you prepare each stem to add its part to the greater whole. You can't just cut stems at any old time. Flowers need to be cut in the early morning or late evening when it's cool and won't cause them to be stressed—otherwise they'll wilt before you even get back to the house. And once you've cut them, you don't just plop them into an arrangement immediately. They need to be given time to rehydrate, rest, and recover before they're ready to be put on display. And honestly, same.

You just can't rush the process it requires. Some things simply need a minute to regroup and gather strength—to drink in what they need before they can stand tall again. You have to strip the foliage. Cut stems at an angle so they can drink deeply. Give blooms enough room to open and take up space. You have to exercise restraint and resist the urge to cram every flower in the bucket just because you grew it. I've done that, and still continue to more than I should. I've tried countless times to fit everything I'd harvested into one arrangement, and nothing had the space to open up to its fullest potential and show off all its glorious, hard-fought beauty. I'm learning, though—and I'm grateful. Curating what to leave *out* is just as important as what to include. Each decision becomes a quiet act of letting beauty lead.

When you leave room for the unexpected, the wild becomes the wow factor. Sometimes you need the structure of a dahlia to hold the eye—and sometimes you need the wild of a celosia to stir it and truly complement it. Though they work on their own, a certain level of enchantment comes when they're placed together.

The best arrangements all have a little tilt. A little wonk. Something off-center that makes you lean in and really *look*. That's where the true magic lives—not in flawless composition, but in curated imperfection. And isn't that where real life mirrors the vase? My story surely becomes a lot more complicated and complex on occasion, but each time I let the unexpected add its own color or texture, I expand as a human and become a whole lot more interesting.

I think about all the arrangements I made and dropped on porches that second summer. They weren't flawless, but they were perfectly unpolished—each carrying a simple, heartfelt message: Someone thought of you. Someone put this together with love and intention. Someone believed you were *worth beauty.*

That's really the heart of it—not chasing perfection, but cultivating beauty in ways that remind us we're all deserving of it. It's about making space for what truly matters, allowing joy to bloom wherever it can. It's about arranging what we've been given into something whole, something holy, something that makes people pause and smile—and maybe even cry a little if they're having one of those days.

Whether it's flowers or friendships, our gardens or our big, hairy, audacious goals, life was never meant to be about getting everything right. It's about shaping a life that sparks joy every time you see it. One that carries peace in knowing you grew what you could and created something beautiful from it. And in the process, acknowledging that you were deserving of beauty, too.

My life has taken more than a few unexpected turns in the last decade—and yet, it's also held more good than I can measure. Looking back, I see it all as part of the arrangement: the messy, the disappointing, the wildly unexpected. Those jagged moments gave my story contrast, depth, and resilience. Without them, it would all be one big sugary-sweet fluff ball of nicety. I do such a disservice to myself and the people in my life when I try to make a tidy, safe bouquet of only the "went as planned or better than hoped for" highlight reel. It's unrelatable, flat, and frankly pretty boring.

Arranging beauty isn't about showing off what's flawless. It's about honoring what held on and stretched toward the sun. What got knocked around, rained on, nearly gave up—and bloomed anyway. The best bouquets—and the best lives—aren't lucky accidents. They're built with intention, heart, some dirt under the nails, and a little chaos in the mix. They're constructed with tenderness and a willingness to let the wild in. They're about gathering what's grown, one imperfect bloom at a time, and always letting beauty lead.

Jeremy let beauty lead when he let me sulk in the Houston airport on our fifth anniversary. We had missed our connecting flight to Belize due to inclement weather delaying our departure from Kansas City, ultimately canceling one of our two nights booked at a gorgeous lodge in the rainforest. I was devastated, but after a stiff margarita and a few minutes in a massage chair, Jeremy suggested we walk around the airport, trying to take photos that made it look like we were already in Belize. It was quintessentially him to find a way to turn this situation around so creatively, and almost instantaneously, I was laughing from my gut as we made an adventure out of our disappointment. Would I have preferred two nights in the rainforest? Of course. Almost seven years later, however, it's one of my favorite moments ever with Jeremy—taking the off-kilter stem of a missed flight and the unexpected bloom of an airport photo scavenger hunt and arranging something unforgettable with them.

Once, letting beauty lead for me meant being brave enough to consider adopting a new furry friend after my first dog passed away. I was completely heartbroken and swore I would "never love again," but I found the quiet of my home after my 90-pound lapdog left to be a void I needed to fill. The nudge to consider opening my heart to another dog started to grow, so one day I went to look at a litter of a breed I knew I wasn't interested in adopting. Just dipping my toe in the pool of curiosity, I figured.

But then I spotted her—a sweet, scared, shiny-as-black-velvet puppy sitting in the bed of a truck. I showed up innocently at what turned out to be Puppypalooza, a rescue event overflowing with multiple abandoned litters needing homes. Everywhere I looked, crates and boxes brimmed with wiggly pups. So much for my carefully laid plan.

I took one look at this girl, the last of her litter, and I was a goner. I knew this four-month-old fluffball needed to come home with me, and thus began a thirteen-year friendship with the best dog I will ever have—my heart dog, Zoey. I took the wilting, weather-worn stem of a broken heart and paired it with the last bud on a mostly-picked plant.

Together, they became the most unexpected bouquet—one I wouldn't have said I was ready for, yet one that arrived exactly on time.

Letting beauty lead doesn't mean chasing what's picture-perfect—it means following the nudge of what's good, true, and alive. It's noticing what stirs your spirit and letting that be the compass, not just the calendar. Beauty, in this sense, is profound. It's a divine invitation wrapped in petals and color and chaos. It whispers, "Pay attention. God's up to something here."

It doesn't demand polish—it asks for presence. You don't have to curate a flawless bouquet or a flawless life to be worthy of love or goodness or light or beauty. You simply need to be honest about what's blooming, what's breaking, and what still needs a minute in a bucket of cold water before it's ready to be seen.

When you let beauty lead, you're not just arranging flowers—you're partnering with the Creator in a tiny act of grace. You're saying, "Look. This grew. Somehow, against all odds, this wild, wonderful thing bloomed—and I'm going to give it a place to shine." And if that's not sacred, I don't know what is.

CHAPTER TWENTY-SEVEN

GRIEF WITH WINGS

Shortly after my mom went to be with Jesus, a bizarre thing started happening. Butterflies began showing up in uncanny ways at uncanny times—more than I ever noticed them before. I don't know what to make of it, so I just accept it as a gift. A holy, mysterious gift. These are the moments I know heaven and earth collide more often than we realize. When the eternal brushes up against the ordinary. When I can feel God's love and presence whispering by way of butterflies, reminding me I am not alone. That not only is my grief not forgotten, but that all will be well.

"All will be well, and all will be well, and all manner of things will be well." – Julian of Norwich

Maybe I started noticing butterflies more because shortly before she passed away, she was one of three women at her church invited to release monarchs on Cancer Survivor Sunday. Maybe I'm just naturally seeing them as I'm outside more, working in the garden. But maybe they have become a way of helping me understand more fully how incredibly thin the veil is between this side and the next, fluttering by as a reminder that she is with me in ways I can't see or understand.

However it's happening, the timing for these visits has been impossible to ignore—and too numerous to count. Take, for example, the time Jeremy took David, JJ, and me to the Miami Dolphins' stadium to see a game after he helped with its renovation. The four of us walked across a very hot asphalt parking lot to the entrance with, I kid you not, a monarch butterfly fluttering in front of us, escorting us the whole way.

In Belize, Jeremy and I finally arrived after missing our connection in Houston, and we took a walk along the river near our lodge. Along the path, a massive owl butterfly appeared and decided to keep us company, landing on each of our arms in turn. It lingered there far longer than any butterfly should—especially on skin that offered no pollen, protection or other reason to stay.

When my twin nieces graduated from high school a few years later, we were sitting high up in the stadium seats when what flew by—not once, but twice? You can sure bet it was a butterfly. I don't know many butterflies who hang out around hot asphalt or the top of stadium seats, so when these visits happen, it sure seems like more than happenstance.

So as my fiftieth birthday approached, as well as the ten-year anniversary of saying goodbye to my sweet mama, I could think of no better place to be than central Mexico, where the monarchs migrate each winter. The thought of being surrounded by millions of monarch butterflies seemed like the closest I could get to heaven itself, so plans were made, flights were booked, and AirBnBs were reserved.

As my second summer garden drew to a close, I watched the monarchs begin their journey south. They feasted on the zinnias and celosia still standing in my beds, even if those blooms were already covered in powdery mildew. But this time it wasn't just one or two—it was eight, nine at a time. The most glorious gift as the season faded. I would watch them for hours, grateful to have a soft place for them to land, and would whisper joyfully, "See you in Mexico!" as they flew away.

As the garden settled in for a long winter's nap—this time tucked under a blanket of leaf mulch and biodegradable cover—I slipped a few larkspur and nigella seeds into the soil. I cut small holes in the cover so they'd have room to breathe and stretch, already dreaming of an earlier spring start in 2025. Some scabiosa had even reseeded itself, and those scrappy little starters were given their own space as well, with frost cloth on standby in case the temperatures dipped too low. The whole idea of "overwintering" still seemed counterintuitive. How could anything thrive in the cold? Yet, the grand experiment piqued my curiosity. I've always had a soft spot for giving *what if* a place to take root.

At the same time, my "Dead To Me List" was growing. Curiosity may have helped a flower through my garden gate, but there was no guarantee it would get a permanent spot. A little assessment was always in order. On the chopping block after 2024? Tulips (as if I need to explain), sunflowers (I know, I know … I live in Kansas, but they just take up too much space in the garden), and strawflower (tried it twice but never loved how they looked in arrangements).

On the short list for "maybe I'll give them one more year" were stock (love the scent, hate how they aren't cut and come again) and anything yellow (don't come at me—I just don't love it in bouquets). There's no rhyme or reason to it; it's simply personal preference. I'm convinced this list will keep evolving as I experiment and try new varieties. So, where sunflowers and strawflowers had once filled certain corners of the garden, I started sketching plans to replace them with ammi, chocolate cosmos, three kinds of rudbeckia, and verbena.

Meanwhile, sale alerts for ranunculus and anemone corms were hitting my inbox, and specialty dahlia tubers were calling my name. Big plans for 2025 were already underway—including that aforementioned garden expansion, of course. However, after long hours in the sun, countless sore backs, and hamstrings that never quite forgave me, I also gave myself permission to tuck in for a while. The garden would rest, and so would I. Soon enough, I'd be ready to begin again, this time with two years of experience under my belt and far more wisdom in my pocket. But first … rest.

Nature teaches us something essential in winter: Rest is part of the cycle. In slowing down, we replenish ourselves for the next season of shining. Monarchs even show us how important it is to prepare for winter and illustrate a necessary cycle in how they rest, restore, and ready themselves for another season.

I used to experience a version of this when I worked as a photographer. Since most of my work was outdoors, winter gave me the gift of a break—time to recharge creatively, tackle the boring-but-necessary things like taxes, and deep-clean everything from my office storage room to my hard drive. Gardening offers me the same pause. A chance to rest my body, sleep a little more, curl up under my favorite blanket, and stay out of the sun for a bit. In 2025, specifically, it even gave me a chance to fly off to Mexico.

Winters are mildly neurotic in Kansas City. We swing from the suffocating heat and humidity of summer to the occasional arctic blast and an overall lack of sunshine come winter. So when January rolled around, flying to Mexico felt like the smartest decision we'd made in years. "We should do this every year!" we said with glee as we boarded the plane to Mexico City.

Thirty-six hours later, I was vomiting in Pujol—one of the world's best restaurants—as norovirus delivered an unwelcome plot twist. Ever watched *Chef's Table* on Netflix? I'd been dreaming of tasting Pujol's legendary molé for years. But by the second course, the meal was over for me. I thought maybe I'd just had bad street tacos the night before, and it would pass. Pass it did … onto Jeremy, who literally ended up in a Mexican hospital for two nights. He was so sick, and I wasn't doing so hot myself. Our carefully curated plans were flushed—well, you get the picture—and the hope of seeing the monarch reserve was fading fast.

At one point, we considered flying straight home, but thankfully things turned around. Ten bags of IV fluids later, Jeremy rallied, and we caught an Uber to the bus station just in time for a ride to San Miguel de Allende. The effort Jeremy made to get me to see the monarchs will never be lost on me.

We landed in the arms of good friends, sipped her homemade chicken noodle soup, and clinked Electrolit poured into wine glasses on the rooftop patio—because nothing says "cheers" quite like hydration salts. A few days later, we finally made our way to El Rosario. Thank God for the horses that carried us most of the way up. Norovirus had left us both so weak we never would've made it otherwise.

We got to the top of the mountain right as the monarchs were waking up. They sleep in clumps, hanging on one another through the night, just high enough in elevation to be out of risk of birds, their greatest predators. We ascended just in time to witness the morning light hit their wings as the sun made its way high enough in the sky.

As they woke, they would fall out of the trees in mass, catching the breeze to take flight, coming at you like a river of wings. The sound alone of thousands of wings flapping will forever register in my mind as one of the most beautiful parts of the whole experience. But the sheer number of them … It was unreal. Each individual butterfly had made a journey of thousands of miles, and there they were—dancing in the morning light, testifying to wonder.

I lay down on the ground right where an opening in the trees gave way to blue skies. I watched as thousands of monarchs flew overhead, a blizzard of beauty that felt otherworldly. It was absolutely breathtaking. Tears slipped down my cheeks, joy spilling over in the only way it could. I simply couldn't process the miracle any other way.

I choose to believe my mom was there with me, somehow. I can't explain it, and I'm not sure I need to. All I know is I that for one brief moment, time folded in on itself. Something eternal brushed up against the ordinary and the veil between heaven and earth grew impossibly thin. In that sliver of grace, I caught the faintest glimpse of what waits for us on the other side. Not the whole picture, but enough to know it's more beautiful than I can begin to imagine.

Grief, I'm learning, doesn't always sit still. Sometimes it grows wings. Sometimes it flutters beside you when you least expect it— at a graduation, a Belizean river walk, or a hot parking lot in Miami. Sometimes it travels hundreds of miles and meets you on a mountaintop in central Mexico, reminding you that love doesn't disappear, it just finds new ways to show up. A brush of wings, a flicker of orange in the sunlight, a moment so breathtaking it hushes even your most practical instincts. You know it when you feel it: *This is sacred.*

I used to think I was gardening just for me—for the color, for the joy. But maybe I'm also gardening to serve. To say with my hands, "You're welcome here. Rest. Be nourished. Take what you need."—whether it's for a butterfly, or a friend, or the broken part of me that still aches for my mom.

A single seed planted.
A single flower offered.
A single butterfly fed.

It sounds small, simple—even forgettable. Yet somehow, in the quiet mystery of it all, I was part of something far bigger than me—woven into the story of movement and migration, of grief giving way to grace. It was a divine exchange. A fragile, winged invitation to say yes to beauty, to stay tender, to believe that love keeps showing up, especially when you need it most.

The mystery is that the smallest things can carry the biggest weight. One zinnia could be part of a monarch's journey. One act of attention, one open patch of earth, one moment of saying yes to beauty could bring me face-to-face with a reminder that love doesn't end—it just changes form.

I think that's part of what keeps me planting. Not the control or the outcome, but the wonder. The not-knowing. The wild possibility that something I nurture in my own backyard might one day take flight—the way butterflies have for me, carrying pieces of my mom forward. It's grief and gift all at once, teaching me that love has a way of continuing its work long after we think the story has ended.

So I'll keep tending my garden. Keep watching for butterflies. Keep believing there's more to this life than we can see—that heaven brushes up against the ordinary more often than we realize. That beauty itself is a kind of benediction. And that somehow, a butterfly might actually be a whisper from eternity saying, *"I'm still here."*

CHAPTER TWENTY-EIGHT

IT WON'T ALL GROW, BUT SOMETHING WILL

When we returned from Mexico, the grand orchestration of seed starting for season three began. I decided to step back a bit on intensity (look who's growing!) and not make my own seed starting mix like some sort of pioneer woman on a homestead in Vermont. Instead, I bought a trusted brand and let it be what it would be. I kind of had to calm down about some of this stuff because shortly after Christmas, I woke from a dream and felt in my soul we needed to sell our A-frame, *The Cocoon Chalet*. It was one of those moments in life where, in the pit of your gut, you know it's a leaning you need to follow—and so after some solid conversations with Jeremy and some time praying about the decision, we ultimately trusted we were being led to make this move.

Looking back, I now see that was but the beginning of a series of surrenders that has been a theme for me in 2025. Letting go of something we had poured so much of ourselves into was painfully bittersweet. We'd carried big dreams of what that space might hold for us in the years ahead, but deep down we knew selling was the right choice—so we did. Then, just a week after closing, I learned my job was coming to an end. Uncertainty seeped into several other things, too, settling like a fog I couldn't quite shake.

I remember looking at my seeds as I tucked them away in my store-bought soil. Each held so much hope of life and beauty to follow. But when you stop and really think of it, most seeds only come from another flower dying. First a blooming, then a letting go—the seed, the final gift. That's the strange and holy rhythm of it all. Growth often begins with surrender. Unexpected beauty often follows loss because nothing new can root itself until something else has released its hold.

It's easy to love the bloom—the showy part. The colorful, fragrant, full-of-life display that turns heads and makes you feel like maybe you *do* know what you're doing after all. But blooms sadly don't last long. They're never really meant to. Their job isn't permanence. Their job is to pour out everything they have—to give until they've got nothing left but the seed—and that tiny, nondescript little speck is what carries the miracle forward.

It's a quiet offering: One form of beauty trading itself in for another. Not immediately. Not without darkness. And the seed doesn't burst into color the second it touches soil. First, it sinks. Then it cracks open. Then it waits. And then—only when it's completely undone from what it once was—does new life emerge.

That's how it works for us, too. We bloom, we give, we love, we create. And then something shifts, ends, breaks, or leaves. We grieve what's been lost. If we're honest, we wonder if we'll ever feel that full again. But buried in that loss—quiet and unseen—is a seed that holds immeasurable potential. Not despite the loss, but *because* of it.

Letting go isn't the end of the story. It's the beginning of a new one. We don't always recognize it while it's happening, but every surrender is an invitation. Every ending—no matter how unwelcome—is a kind of planting. A letting go that makes space for something else to rise. I used to think some versions of loss meant I had done something wrong—miscalculated, missed a step, held on too tight. The simple truth is, though, that the right yes at one point might not be the right yes forever. So what if letting go is the very act that makes room for what is?

That's what I was experiencing in 2025. I didn't know it yet, but the seeds I was planting were mirroring something much deeper.

The cabin we let go of. The job I hadn't seen ending so quickly. The swirl of uncertainty around everything else. The numbness in my right hand even returned—that which had ended my photography career seven years earlier. All of it felt like a very layered, unwelcome undoing—and I didn't like it one bit. But what if all that letting go would divinely prepare me for what was coming?

So there I was, still reeling from all the deep, soul-level pruning 2025 was presenting, and somehow I was also starting seeds like it was the most normal thing in the world. Emotional chaos? Midlife (career) crisis? Sure. But also … it was time to plant snapdragons. In store-bought seed starting soil, no less.

"Let it be what it will be," I told myself, in a tone that was 50% serenity and 50% mild exhaustion. And sure, I still hovered over those trays like a nervous mother. Don't judge me. You try casually ignoring hundreds of tiny promises of life that may or may not depend on your precise misting technique.

But honestly, it felt right to hold it all a little more loosely this season. The seeds would do what they were going to do. And if they didn't, I'd start over. Or maybe just buy seedlings from someone who had more capacity than I did right then.

Somehow, planting still felt like the exact right thing to do. Not because I had a master plan (I didn't) or because I was in full control (I wasn't)—but because choosing beauty over spiraling or stalling is sometimes the best move you've got. When the future feels like one giant shrug emoji and you don't know what's next, quietly tucking a seed into soil feels like whispering, "I trust that beauty will come again."

So I got to work. I planted the seeds. I plugged in the heat mats and turned on the grow lights. I pulled out the ranunculus corms and the anemone bulbs. I tucked them into slightly moistened soil and kept them in the dark, just the way they like it when they're sprouting.

"I'm in the dark, too, guys," I said as I checked on them. "But maybe we can find our way together." Honestly, it felt like a team-building exercise with my plants. They were silent. I brought the awkward emotional oversharing. Classic.

I threw out some more poppy seeds just in case, not sure if the ones I put out before a big snowstorm that winter were actually going to sprout. Hope can be stubborn, and I was holding onto it real tight. I kept repeatedly trying to summon life where there was a void, hoping it might return the favor.

To really up the stakes, I bought five new raised beds and nine cubic yards of specialty soil mix—because apparently, I cope with existential unease by expanding infrastructure. I needed space for the 28 specialty dahlias I ordered in October (no regrets) and my 12 favorite zinnia varieties (which I can now list from memory like they're my kids). We pulled up more sod, installed new fencing to make the whole setup a bit more permanent and more HOA compliant, then placed two Adirondack chairs in the middle of it all—right between the 2023 and 2025 spaces—so we could sit amongst the blooms and soak in the ever-expanding beauty as the season unfolded.

The spring was glorious. The ranunculus and anemone flourished. Larkspur and nigella made their beautiful debut. So much in the 2023 garden space came alive again. It all appeared to be thriving—until I looked at the new raised beds. That's when things got weird.

The zinnias germinated and sprouted. The dahlias eventually broke the surface. But then … everything just stopped. It was like someone hit pause on the whole garden expansion, and no amount of fish emulsion could get it going again. Suddenly, I was having PTSD flashbacks to our first summer when we planted out the itty-bitty, teeny-weeny seedlings. Why were they not growing?! Ugh! Jesus, take the wheel— and my garden trowel.

I called the soil company we had purchased from and followed the directions they gave me. Nothing happened. I asked other flower friends what to do and followed their suggestions. Nothing happened. And then all of a sudden, my precious specialty dahlias, which I had worked so hard to acquire, started dying. All that effort, all that hope— and nothing to show for it but shriveled stems and disappointment. My garden's crown jewels had become compost in waiting.

Meanwhile, I had an aphid breakout in my ranunculus patch and literally went shopping for ladybugs. Did you know you can buy ladybugs in bulk? *You can buy live ladybugs in bulk.* They will munch, munch, munch on those aphids like they are fresh caramel popcorn—hundreds a day per ladybug! I still find this equal parts magical and vaguely terrifying. I'm not sure I'll ever see a little kid in a ladybug costume at Halloween quite the same.

At this point, I started telling people that gardening felt like sorcery disguised as a granny hobby (kidding, of course). It was a funny way to express my overwhelm because one flower needed *this*, and another needed *that*. One had to be planted in *snow*, and another couldn't go outside until the soil hit 70 degrees. One needed ladybugs to control what was attacking it, and one apparently benefited from a *diluted molasses spray* to raise its brix (aka sugar) level and make pests leave it alone?! I evidently should also avoid planting when Mercury is in retrograde. Oy vey.

I bought a soil test kit from the nursery to check pH, nitrogen (N), phosphorus (P), potassium (K) ... all the letters. Still nothing. Just to cover all bases, I also sent off a soil sample to be professionally analyzed. They sent back a 3-page PDF with more mineral data than I knew what to do with. I had entered a realm I was not prepared for: advanced flower science. This wasn't gardening anymore. It felt like the final scene of *E.T.*, only instead of a glowing spaceship, it was me waving a pH meter over my soil, whispering, "Stay with me, buddy."

When it all comes down to it, soil is everything in gardening. It's the heartbeat of the whole operation—the place where every possibility begins, or withers. The longer I do this, the more I understand: Good soil isn't just a nice bonus, it's the foundation. The whole dang house is built on it. You can have the fanciest tools, the prettiest seeds, and the most aesthetically pleasing grid layout in the neighborhood, but if your soil is trash? So is your garden.

I'm still trying to figure it all out. Still the student, still Googling "what does nitrogen deficiency look like?" at 11:47 p.m., but unless I inherit an entire research staff and a personal greenhouse, I'm probably always going to be troubleshooting.

In a desperate attempt to revive my raised beds, I tried everything I could think of. I amended the soil with everything short of a blood sacrifice—

worm castings, composted mushroom yadayada, and liquified fish guts that smelled like a crime scene. I added "earthworms" to my actual shopping list. I ordered "beneficial nematodes" online like some kind of woman dabbling in black-market underground organisms. All of it in the name of trying to create soil that would finally sustain life.

When nothing seemed to work, I decided to do what all hopeful, half-exhausted gardeners do when faced with floral tragedy: I started digging things up. I gently lifted any tuber that hadn't rotted and walked it over to the 2023 garden bed, my trusty old patch of good, lived-in soil that had proven itself before. Like an ICU for struggling dahlias, it became my last-ditch incubator—my rescue ward for anything showing even a faint pulse.

And … that brings us to the present. I don't expect blooms from those dang beds this year, but if they show any sign of life—a bit of foliage, a stem stretching just a little—I'll take it as a win. And maybe, just maybe, if I give the raised beds a full year to breathe, to marinate in buffalo manure and cover crop, to let the microbial soil rave kick into full gear, 2026 might be their year. They might actually be ready. Until then, I'm choosing to believe that if nothing else grows in those beds this summer, at least I'm growing something that really matters: hope.

Hope is an essential part of gardening. If this book hasn't made that painfully obvious, I don't know what else to tell you. But hope, once it roots, doesn't stay confined to places like those new raised beds. It has this sneaky way of spilling into everything—your work, your relationships, your grief, and even your outlook on an increasingly chaotic world.

Did I start to see the good that came from letting go of our beloved A-frame? I sure dang did. Did I stumble into a new job in the most unexpected of ways that made saying goodbye to one I loved a little less of a bummer? Absolutely. Is my hand still numb? Unfortunately, but I now have an occupational therapist, and ulnar nerve glides are part of my daily routine, right alongside watering and deadheading.

There will always be something. Always. No matter how much you learn or how much compost you throw at a problem. The weather will surprise you. The pests will be pests. The soil won't cooperate. Your favorite tuber might shrivel like a forgotten raisin. Something will go sideways—guaranteed. But there is always a way forward. Maybe not immediately. Maybe not this season. But eventually.

Here's the thing: You get to keep trying. It's honestly as simple as that. As I look back on everything—the mistakes, the wins, the powdery mildew and the panic-purchased ladybugs—I'm reminded of what my friend April said way back at the start: *Something will grow. It won't all grow, but something will.*

You get to believe that what you're doing matters. You get to keep fighting for beauty. Even if it takes buffalo manure, a bag of beneficial nematodes, and a homemade garlic–cayenne concoction that smells like regret. That's what gardeners do. We fight for what's beautiful. And that scrappy, tender, relentless fight could actually change everything—most significantly, *you*.

CHAPTER TWENTY-NINE

SAY THE QUIET YES

I'm knee-deep in season three of My Grand Suburban Micro Flower Farming Experiment™. The adventures are still unfolding, and the verdict is very much TBD with this year's cocktail of weird weather and stubborn soil. Will the ladybugs prevail in The Great Aphid War of 2025? Will the heat dome we're living under torch everything to a crisp before it even has a chance? Will the dahlias bloom or bail? Will *anything* grow from those flipping raised beds? At all? Who knows? I sure don't, but I also can't wait to see.

It's easy to poke fun at all the mistakes I made along the way these last few years. The more I learn, the more obvious they become—like dandelions in a spring lawn, popping up everywhere. Yet, somehow, beauty bloomed. Not everything. Not perfectly. But enough to be proud of, enough to keep going, and more than enough to prove that participation matters more than perfection.

I'm grateful I started when I did—scared, unsure, and completely unqualified. I'm grateful I jumped in and figured it out along the way. I didn't wait for the perfect plan, the "right" tools, or a certificate in soil biology. I just listened to my heart, followed the nudge, and learned as I went. I've now watched more flower videos on YouTube than any functioning adult should probably admit. I've logged more trips to the nursery's "Garden Pharmacy" than I can count. I've learned more about soil health than anyone—especially David and JJ—ever wanted to hear (sorry, guys).

But here's what matters most: I've never felt more alive.

This journey has brought joy to my life that I didn't even know I was missing. It's unlocked parts of myself I hadn't yet met, and now I believe—wholeheartedly and unequivocally—that I was meant for this. My heart was truly designed for this. And I know in my bones the real blooming has been in me, not just in the flowers. That's a level of goodness that sneaks up on you when you're elbow-deep in dirt or watching a dahlia unfurl for the first time. It's the kind of joy that feels like an exhale you didn't know you needed to take.

I've witnessed magic bloom from literal dirt. I've had the gift of sharing that magic with neighbors, friends, and strangers online. And when people told me they felt inspired to try it themselves? Stop it right now. That's the proverbial cherry on top I never saw coming. The truth is, however, that beauty gives birth to more beauty. Courage gives birth to more courage. And even the quietest act of bravery sends ripples farther than you'll ever know.

When I consider how much goodness and beauty have come simply because I chose to say yes to curiosity and listen to that quiet voice in my heart, I shudder to consider the alternative. What if I had told myself I wasn't ready? What if I convinced myself I needed more time to research or needed to be more qualified before I began? What if I chose to be more afraid of failure than to believe I might actually be able to do this? What if I thought I wasn't worth the risk? What if I just ignored the pull and turned on Netflix? I could have missed *all of it*. I *would* have missed all of it. I think about all the color, growth, and magic that would have stayed dormant, and it wrecks me a little.

Please hear me when I say this: Don't miss *your* moment because you're afraid to start.

Don't keep your own blooming on the back burner until everyone else is settled and satisfied. You are not required to be the emotional air traffic controller of everyone else's chaos before you earn your shot at joy. You don't have to be the martyr, the fixer, or the one who makes life easier for everyone else while telling yourself your dreams can wait. They shouldn't. They have most likely waited long enough.

You are not selfish for wanting something for yourself.
You are not indulgent for dreaming big.
You are not foolish for hoping again.

You are not too much.
You are not too late.
You are just in time.

So go on and risk a little. Plant the thing. Start the thing. Take up your dang space without apology. Because *you are worth it*—even if the only thing that grows is your own joy.

This cut flower garden of mine used to simply be grass. The kind people edge with pride and mow diagonally for the visual flair. And though I know many go cuckoo for Coco Puffs over a beautiful lawn, it doesn't hold a candle to the hundreds of square feet of blooms that now stand in its place. I walk among rows of flowers I nurtured from seed—color and fragrance and texture exploding from what was once just turf. I watch bees and butterflies land gently on petals, resting before heading off to pollinate or migrate. Some are heading all the way to Mexico. Others are making something bloom right here at home. All of it, a holy sight.

And it all started because I listened to a tug quietly calling for my attention.

So let me ask you: What's tugging at *your* heart right now?

What's the thing you've buried under logistics and laundry and to-do lists? What's the quiet dream you've told yourself is silly or selfish or not for "someone like you"? What have you already decided isn't possible, before you even gave yourself the chance to try?

Please hear me: You are worth the risk. You are worth the chance.

Don't talk yourself out of it before you even begin. You don't need a five-year plan. You (probably) don't need an LLC. You don't even need to know the end goal right now. For today, just say "This is what I dream of." Then, figure out what the next right step is and take it.

Because your joy matters.

I believe more than anything that I experience the Divine in joy. God meets me in those bone-deep, soul-lit-up, goosebumps-on-your-forearm moments when I'm fully alive. When you're doing the thing you were made to do—even if you're just beginning, even if no one else notices—it changes you. And it changes the people around you, too.

There's something profound waiting for you in your beginning—in your brave yes to joy. We are not meant to measure life only by productivity, as if efficiency were the highest good. We are meant to feel wonder and to chase curiosity. To even just try things simply because they make us come alive. Even if we're bad at them or if no one else understands. Yes, even if they cost us something. Curiosity is not a weed to be plucked—it's a seed of possibility waiting to be tended.

Because you're not just a consumer of life—you're a co-creator. I believe that's part of what it means to be made in the image of God. But even if you don't share that belief, you've probably felt it—that nudge inside that longs to build, make, grow, or express. Co-creators respond to that nudge. They plant, write, dance, start, stumble, and learn. And they keep going, even when the soil feels barren, the dream feels foolish, or when nothing seems to be working.

Flowers have taught me to always keep growing—
to bloom even if it feels too late,
to try again when the season changes,
to trust that the tiniest seed can hold the biggest transformation.

No matter your age, your background, your resources, your health, your history—it is not too late. There is *always* a way. Please don't doubt this. Doubt kills more dreams than failure ever will.

When you find the guts to say yes and you take that first trembling step, I'd bet anything that one day you'll look back—just as I do now, three years into my own yes—and see all the goodness and joy your bravery made possible. More beauty than weeds. More blooms than what withered. You might even begin to see where that dream of yours first took root—with little boys playing catch in the front yard or a grandma taking you on a forced tour of her roses. And that all along, you yourself were blooming. Right in the middle of your life. Right in the middle of the mess. Right when you weren't sure you had it in you.

So listen to your heart. Listen to the nudge calling you forward. Close your eyes and imagine the beauty waiting on the other side of that first seed, first word, first flight, first brushstroke. Whatever it is—whatever is whispering your name—you'll figure it out as you go.

Stop waiting.
Stop doubting.
Say yes to the dream tugging at you.

Because a braver, bolder, more alive version of you is eagerly waiting to bloom—and it's the most beautiful version of you yet.

ALWAYS KEEP GROWING

May you plant the things that scare you—
the projects you're underqualified for,
the dreams you can't shake,
the "what ifs" that won't leave you alone.

May you pull the weeds—
the doubts, the drama, the energy vampires,
and every voice that whispers you're not enough.
(Into the compost pile they go. Good riddance.)

May you water the sparks of joy
that feel too frivolous to matter—
because (and this is important)
those are usually the ones that do.

And may you notice the blooms—
the tiny victories, the stubborn latecomers,
the blossoms so beautiful you forget to breathe for a second.
Each one is proof that your showing up wasn't wasted.

When it feels messy, keep tending.
When it feels small, keep trusting.
When it feels impossible, keep showing up anyway.
Growth often looks like chaos before it looks like beauty.

You are not behind.
You are not too late.
You are not disqualified by your past missteps.
You are exactly where you need to be to begin again.

So here's to ripping up the lawn,
to planting way too many seeds,
to laughing at yourself, crying when you need to,
and celebrating every ridiculous, miraculous bloom along the way.

Because growth doesn't end with one season,
or one dream, or one "success."
It keeps unfolding—
messy and unpredictable and sometimes a little extra—
always inviting you, over and over,
to become more fully yourself.

Rip it up, plant it wild, bloom like crazy—
and let the world be better *because you did*.

WITH ALL MY GRATITUDE

This book would not exist without a small army of people who cheered me on, talked me off ledges, and tolerated way too many flower metaphors in casual conversation.

To Jeremy: Who knew holding a shovel could look like a love story? Thank you for being my calm in the chaos, for troubleshooting Adobe, and helping me tend to flower beds amidst it all. None of this would be possible without you. You've shown me, time and time again, what partnership really looks like. I love you most, avocado toast.

To David and JJ: Thank you for every hole you reluctantly dug, every bag of mulch you lugged, and for not rolling your eyes too hard while I turned the yard into a flower circus. You may not have realized the role you played in helping me discover this passion of mine, but I am forever grateful for it and all the ways you have changed my life, making it more beautiful than I could have ever dreamed.

To my friends and family: Thank you for nodding politely while I launched into passionate monologues about compost, powdery mildew, and dahlias like they were breaking news alerts. Your patience deserves a medal. And to all the people who told me over the years, *"I can't wait to read your book someday"*—joke's on me, because I never actually intended to write one. You planted a seed with your encouragement and belief, and over time it took root and grew into this. I'm grateful for the push.

To MK, my editor and dear friend: You are the unsung hero here. Thank you for shaping this book into something truer, tighter, and braver than I could have pulled off alone. Without you, half of this story would still be languishing in draft form. I am beyond grateful you gently but consistently pushed me to finish. Each step of the way, you helped me stay funny and coherent—the truest proof of your genius—while always making me believe this was worth writing.

To Anna, Julie, and Stefani—my brilliant beta readers: Thank you for combing through early drafts, for your honesty, and for helping me see the places that needed some pruning. You made this book stronger without once dimming its heart.

To my fellow gardeners and flower farmers—in real life and online: You've been a constant source of inspiration and wisdom. You each assured me in your own ways that I could figure this out little by little. Special thanks to Noella, Angela, Ashley, Meg, Colleen, Heather and Ronni, my Zone 6b role models.

To my Aunt Carol: Thank you for standing in where my mom would have been. You were the first to hear most of these chapters and became a living exclamation point in her absence, celebrating each sentence in ways that made the void feel less empty. I love you so.

And to my mom: You are stitched into every page of this book, every butterfly I greet in my garden, and every brave yes I've whispered into the world since you've been gone. I hope I've made you proud.

Finally, to you—the reader holding this book: Thank you for giving this first-time author a chance. I don't take it lightly that you've let my words take up space in your brain. My hope is that this book makes you laugh, maybe cry, and definitely risk planting your own "what if." The world is waiting for the beauty that will come from your brave yes. I can't wait to see it.

TO PONDER, JOURNAL, OR DISCUSS WITH FRIENDS

---

1. What surprised you most about Kelly's journey from new stepmom to micro flower farmer? Did it mirror any season of your own life where you were learning something new or starting from scratch?

2. Throughout the book, Kelly often finds meaning in her mistakes. Which story resonated most with you—and what did it make you reflect on in your own life?

3. Grief and growth show up side by side a lot in Kelly's story. How have beauty and loss intertwined in your own?

4. Several chapters explore control and surrender—plans vs. what actually grows. Where in your life are you being invited to loosen your grip or trust the process?

5. Kelly describes creativity and gardening as acts of co-creation. How does that idea land with you? Where do you see collaboration with something bigger than yourself in your own work or life?

6. In seasons of waiting—whether for blooms, dreams, or healing—what helps you stay hopeful?

7. Which metaphor, garden lesson, or life story lingered with you most after reading? Why do you think it stuck?

8. The garden in this story evolves every year — wild, unpredictable, and oftentimes full of surprises. What in your own life has taught you to embrace change or imperfection more freely?

9. Kelly's garden reminds her that growth often happens beyond her control. When have you witnessed goodness or grace take root in your life without your planning or striving?

10. This book ends with a call to "say the quiet yes"—to listen to the small tug of curiosity inside you. What dream, desire, or next step is quietly tugging at you right now? And what might it look like to trust that nudge and say yes?

If you've made it this far, thank you for spending time in these stories. My hope is that something here nudged you toward beauty, bravery, or a little more wonder in your own life.

If you're reading *Beyond the Bloom* with friends, a book club, or just a group that loves deep conversation and good snacks, I'd love to cheer you on from afar. Tag me on Instagram @iamkellycrabb or use #BeyondTheBloom to share what's growing in your life as a result of reading this. I'd be honored to see how these words take root in your corner of the world.

GARDENER, WRITER, OCCASIONAL HOT MESS

Kelly Crabb believes beauty is found in both blossoms and the layers of life. She's spent the last few years chronicling what her suburban flower garden has taught her about courage, grief, and the audacity of growth. Before writing, Kelly built a twenty-year career in photography, which gave her a love for noticing light, color, and detail—the same things that now show up in her garden and her words.

She stumbled into gardening the same way she's stumbled into most good things in life—by saying yes before she felt ready (her signature move). She believes bravery is less about big leaps and more about planting tiny seeds you're not sure will grow. Her flower beds became a classroom for resilience, humor, and hope, and her stories now weave together the reverent and the ridiculous in equal measure.

Kelly makes her home in Overland Park, Kansas, with her husband Jeremy, their rescue pups, and an ever-expanding collection of flowers that rarely stay where she plants them. Their two boys, David and JJ, are still her favorite things to watch grow—even as they stretch their own roots beyond home. When she's not in her garden, Kelly loves seeing the world with Jeremy, the scratch of a needle on vinyl, and laughing from her gut as much as possible.